SECRETS OF STYLISTS

STYLIST
SECRETS O
STYLIST

SASHA CHARNIN MORRISO
FOREWORD BY GRACE MIRABEL

SECRETS O
STYLIST
SECRETS O
STYLIST

AN INSIDER'S GUIDE TO STYLING THE STAF

SECRETS

CHRONICLE BOO
SAN FRANCISCO

STYLIST

SECRETS OF STYLISTS

AN INSIDER'S GUIDE TO STYLING THE STARS

SASHA CHARNIN MORRISON
FOREWORD BY GRACE MIRABELLA

Library of Congress Cataloging-in-Publication Data:

Morrison, Sasha Charnin.
     The secrets of stylists : an insider's guide to styling the stars
     / Sasha Charnin Morrison.
               p. cm.
     ISBN 978-0-8118-7465-6 (pbk.)
     1. Fashion—United States—Vocational guidance. 2. Cloth-
     ing trade—United States—Vocational guidance. 3. Motion
     picture actors and actresses—Clothing—United. States. I.
     Title.

     TT507.M676 2011
     746.9'2023—dc22

2010023643

Manufactured in China

Designed by **Ayako Akazawa**

10 9 8 7 6 5 4 3 2 1

Chronicle Books LLC
680 Second Street
San Francisco, California 94107
www.chroniclebooks.com

CONTENTS

FOREWORD

BY GRACE MIRABELLA

WHEN I WAS EDITOR IN CHIEF OF *VOGUE* from 1971 to 1988, there was no such thing as a "celebrity stylist." Instead, there were fashion editors and editorial stylists. Back then, almost everything was done behind the scenes. Then in the 1990s, things started to change. Hiring someone else to put your looks together became acceptable, and stylists came out from behind the curtains.

Dressing has changed dramatically since I was at *Vogue*. More and more women (not just celebrities) need help finding clothes and putting looks together. Designers may have a lot of influence, but prices are still high. Looking good has become more challenging. The components of style aren't easy to find. We miss Yves Saint Laurent. We miss style as a consistency in dressing. A way of "presenting ourselves" seems lost. Yet today, it seems like everyone is a fashion authority and everyone wants to be a stylist. Every woman watching the Oscars comments knowingly on how each actress looks. "Dreadful again this year." "Does anyone help her?" But it takes a lot of discipline and experience to become a stylist. It's not a career that you can just fall into.

I got my start at *Vogue* in 1954. In 1962, Diana Vreeland arrived. She was a fascinating woman who changed everything we knew about fashion and everything we did with clothing, shoes, accessories, and makeup. She was an incredible teacher—and incredibly demanding. As I said, back then stylists were unheard of. Instead, we fashion editors pulled the clothes for shoots. For big location trips, clothes were first shown to Mrs. V in her office. The fashion editors dressed the models, accessorized them, and then took Polaroids of the looks. We then wrote notes in the Polaroid book emphasizing exactly how the clothes were to be worn for the shoot, how things were to be accessorized, even describing the tilt of the hat. Everything, every tiny detail mattered. It was a grueling process but it taught me how to create a look, how to style.

I don't think of myself as a fashion maven and I never made proclamations about fashion. What matters to me is creating a certain reality with looks. The clothes and the women wearing them have to look great, move beautifully. I rarely used fashion as a joke. The best example of this is fashion in the hands of photographers such as Irving Penn, Richard Avedon, Helmut Newton, and Deborah Turbeville—each one is so different from the others, yet each created sensuous, stylish, sexy, alluring looks. Look carefully at their photographs. Take the clothes apart piece by piece and put them back on the model. See how important each piece is and how together they deliver an authentic message of style. Learning to create looks is difficult. Part of it is instinct. But quite a bit is learned. That's the beauty of this book. In it, Sasha Charnin Morrison takes the place of a teacher, when you're not lucky enough to have a terribly demanding first boss with an incredible presence as I did in Diana Vreeland.

Fashion is in Sasha's blood. I first met her when she was thirteen. Even at that young age she was living and breathing fashion. Her step-mother, Jade Hobson, was the accessories editor at *Vogue*. Sasha always wanted to be involved in stories we were producing, whether it was dashing off to pick up Jade's black lace top from her closet to make a perfect Steven Meisel accessories shot, or laying out shoes on the floor of a van on another Jade shoot. After *Vogue*, I started *Mirabella*. Sasha worked with me and Jade there. She did everything that needed doing—a new magazine needs that energy. Sasha became a key player as model editor, booking models, working with celebrity press agents, collaborating with the fashion editors doing the sittings. She is savvy, amusing, and very much aware of what's around her. She knows just about everything there is to know about being a stylist and working in front of and behind the camera.

The world of styling is a small and independent world. You have to make decisions for yourself: figure out how to find the job, what to wear and not to wear, how to act, speak, present yourself, take initiative, and build a clientele. *Secrets of Stylists* will motivate you. It will make you laugh, groan, smile, and nod knowingly. Use it and learn from it. Sasha has interviewed the people on the front lines—those who started at the bottom, who work with amazing talent today, and who tell it like it is.

INTRODUCTION

In today's world, stylists have become almost as important and as powerful as the person they're dressing. Stylists work with legends (both the celebrity and fashion sorts), and they're privy to fashion news and trends six to twelve months before the rest of the world. Stylists are the ones who get to choose the best new glamorous gowns for their clients. And they even have their own language, imbued with initialisms, when the beauty of a dress is too intense for full words: "OMG" (oh my God), "OOC" (out of control), "TBW" (to be worn), and "TDF" (to die for). (See Edu-ma-cate Me! on page 162 for more acronyms and industry terms.) What's not to love?

Thanks to TV channels like Bravo and MTV, and shows such as *Project Runway, The Rachel Zoe Project, The Hills, The City,* and *What Not to Wear,* there's almost no such thing as *behind the scenes* anymore. Suddenly the stylists *are* the stars. Television shows and webisodes about styling paint a seductive picture: Stylists travel to Paris, get driven around in an Escalade from appointment to appointment, reap the benefits of amazing swag, and go to Mr. Chow or Katsuya on the arm of a celebrity and bask in their reflected glow. Yes, this can happen. But the job is actually very hard work and very little play—especially in the beginning.

The good news, though, is that anyone can apply to this business. There's no degree necessary. A high-profile stylist once told me, "You don't need to be scholarly smart and you don't need any formal qualifications." What you do need is a thick skin and a few years as an assistant to get your start. Most of the training will be on the job, with very little hand-holding. The trick is knowing how to apply yourself and how to get the tools and training necessary to succeed.

And that's why I wrote this book—to show you how to make it in this business. In the pages ahead, I'll explain the daily ins and outs of the job, without sparing any of the gory details. I'll give you the lowdown on everything from how to land your first gig to how to survive in this competitive industry and how to cope with both the Sybils and the saints. I've even sprinkled in exclusive private photos so that you can get a real look inside the world of stylists.

My fascination with fashion began when I was in cloth diapers. I basically grew up in a celebrity circus. Raised in Greenwich Village during the late 1960s, I was always surrounded by people with strong personal style. The dawning of the Age of Aquarius was happening in my backyard every day in Washington Square Park.

My parents were show business hippies who looked insanely groovy, were great shoppers, and dressed to the nines with little money. They taught me that style doesn't have a price tag. The key is learning how to work with what you have—how to put it all together—and not be afraid to stand out as an individual. My mother is and was an incredible fashion force and influence. She always dressed me in chic clothing that she picked up in Paris and London and went out of her way to make me look different. My father was a great shopper as well: suede jackets, furs, washed-out jeans, moccasin slip-ons. He used to schlep me over to a store on Broadway called Robbins Men's Store, which had bins filled with a particular T-shirt he loved and tube socks that didn't have stripes. I use to adore watching how he was so into it. And he was straight!

When I was twelve, I met one of my earliest mentors: my father's girlfriend (my parents had split by then), Jade Hobson. She was this incredible glamazon who worked at *Vogue* magazine. Could you die? I had read *Seventeen, Mademoiselle, Harper's Bazaar,* and *Vogue* religiously— even at that early age—and was obsessed with knowing every detail of a fashion shoot: the models' names, the photographers, the clothing, the locations.

One day in 1977, Jade invited me to a photo shoot. I wore a white thermal shoulder-padded dress with a big logo on the front from Parachute, a hugely influential fashion boutique from the 1980s, and mesh sling-back heels by Sacha London in Day-Glo pink. (Sounds positively disgusting to me now, but I thought I looked outstanding.) The shoot was in Union Square at the studio of the famous photographer Chris von Wangenheim. What I recall most clearly from the entire experience was the drama that ensued when the celebrity model rebuffed the hair and makeup team even though *Vogue* had booked two of the best in the business. The star refused to let them touch her. She kicked them both out of her dressing room and did the work herself. She emerged glorious, but this type of behavior was unheard of, particularly on a *Vogue* shoot. I loved it. I was smitten with the screaming, the flurry of activity in the studio, the theatrics of the entire ordeal.

Later, when I was invited to the *Vogue* fashion closet one afternoon after school, I fell in lust. I couldn't believe how many shoes, handbags, belts, scarves, and other clothes were packed into this little closet on Madison Avenue. I didn't know how the whole enterprise worked, but whatever it was—I wanted it. And so began my career.

Around 1982, I made friends with Michael Peters, who co-choreographed *Dreamgirls* on Broadway and collaborated with Michael Jackson on the "Beat It" and "Thriller" videos. At some point, Michael Peters needed authentic-looking runaway teenage hookers for a music video titled "Love Is a Battlefield." So I went in to audition as a dancer (a.k.a. hooker), wearing a sweatshirt with a decal that read *Maybe* in French on the front and *Never* on the back, white snow-leopard jeans, and yellow Norma Kamali high heels. Another hot look (ha!). But based on that look, I won the

small role of Teenage Runaway Hooker #1. After the audition, the costume designer asked me where I got my chic streetwalker duds. I told her about the boutique on Columbus Avenue called Acrobat, where I had been working, which sold progressive French and Italian labels. I invited the costume designer to come with me to the boutique and buy some stuff. She did. In fact, most of Pat Benatar's style in the video was inspired by my look the day of the audition. I may not have scored a big role, but I was flattered that the production team used me as their style muse.

While my fellow NYU classmates planned their post-college careers in acting, directing, playwriting, psychology, advertising, public relations, or working on a kibbutz, I went into fashion, styling, and seeing my work on beautiful people. In 1985, while I was studying costume and scenic design, I landed a job assisting costume designer Kevin

WHO WORE IT BETTER?

Sasha, Jane Street, New York, 1970 (left); my mom, Jane Street, New York, 1970 (right)

1. Sasha at 3, Jane Street / 2. Sasha, Mexico, 1971 / 3. Sasha, "Montenegro Style," Fire Island, 1967 / 4. Sasha, pageboy cut / 5. Sasha and Mom, Haiti, 1980 / 6. Sasha and Mom, White Suit, 1971 / 7. Sasha's 25th birthday with Mom / 8. Sasha and brother, Randy, 1982 / 9. Sasha and Martin—Daddy / 10. Mom at pool in Williamsburg, Brooklyn / 11. My parents— together in a picture!—Acapulco / 12. Sasha, Bar, Madison Avenue House, 1978 / 13. Will and Sasha, Sasha's birthday, 1993 / 14. *Mirabella*, circa 1989 / 15. Sasha, *Seventeen*, 1993 / 16. Sasha, Madonna Hair, 1990

Dornan and being a dresser to Madonna for a play called *Goose and TomTom*, costarring Sean Penn, Harvey Keitel, Lorraine Bracco, and Barry Miller. I was sent out to find mafioso gold pinkie rings, fur-trimmed '50s-style sweaters, capri leggings, Fogal back-seamed silk stockings, red pumps, and black and white wife-beater tank tops (Madonna loved these tops, and I got her a men's small because the concept of women wearing men's undergarment silhouettes wasn't even on the fashion radar).

Madonna was in her "Papa Don't Preach" incarnation, with short blond hair, porcelain skin, black bustier, capris, and ballerina slippers. When I met her, I was impressed by how she knew exactly what she wanted and how in control of everything she was. She was probably the biggest star on the planet—still is to this day—and I'm so grateful I had the chance to work for her. When she asked for something special, I borrowed some gold chains from the *Vogue* fashion closet for her. I also borrowed some red Vittorio Ricci pumps and a leopard-print Norma Kamali coat. She seemed to embrace the stuff, and it was a trip to see her wear all of it.

What I loved most about her was how she knew what worked for her. Even though she had collaborated on and off with stylist Maripol (who was responsible for the stretch silver bracelets, star earrings, and all that rubber), Madonna was an individual who created her own trends. For instance, she cut her tights and swaddled the legs around her head, making some crazy head wrap. I copied her. I did everything she did.

After those amazing experiences, I was hooked. I decided to work in fashion full-time. I followed my true love for magazines and have since worked at many high-fashion glossies, including *Vanity Fair, Mirabella, Seventeen, Elle, Harper's Bazaar,* and *Allure.* It was when I got to *Harper's Bazaar* and worked on a shoot with R&B star Lauryn Hill that everything started coming together for me.

We were shooting her for a cover and inside story. As a fashion market editor who handled clothing from specific cities, I was asked to call in a head-to-toe "look" that was being shown on the runways in Paris. We had racks and racks of gowns, tank tops, furs, and denim for Lauryn and our *Harper's Bazaar* stylist to choose from. But the list of people defining Lauryn's specific look didn't end there. We also had a visit from Lauryn's personal styling team: one stylist, Deborah Waknin, handled only the looks that would be photographed for magazine covers, while another stylist, Tameka Foster (Usher's ex-wife), was responsible for styling the interior shots. This is when I first realized that styling celebrities was an actual job and that celebrities hired stylists specifically to dress them for personal or professional events.

I worked in the world of glossy fashion mags until 2006, when I went to work at the famous celebrity gossip bible *Us Weekly.* It may seem like a crazy move, but nobody told me I was nuts. Everyone knew how much I loved this particular magazine and genre. To be working at a place that combines everything I'm obsessed with is a dream come true. I love to dish about celebrities, read about them, study their clothes and hairstyle changes, and track how many Louis Vuitton bags they own or were gifted by eager paparazzi. In my job at *Us Weekly,* I style covers and fashion features in the magazine. Each time I get an e-mail blast about a celebrity wearing the latest Marchesa gown or a new Jimmy Choo or a piece of fine jewelry from Chopard, my immediate response is: *Who put her in this?* Meaning, *Who was the brain behind this stunning vision* or, conversely, *Who put her in this heinous creation?*

But the job of styling isn't always as glossy as the paper it's printed on. The sob stories about being treated like last year's Versace or complete crap by certain celebrities are unabashedly true. We stylists have lost years of sleep

"Love is a Battlefield" video (left); my step-major-mother Jade Hobson (middle);
Mom, me, and Michael Peters, who cast me in "Love is a Battlefield" (right)

stressing about whether a dress would arrive on time, cried our eyes out over missing or damaged sequins and bugle beads, cleaned out prop kits for models who needed to pee when there was no potty available. We've wept to FedEx on the weekends when boxes were mistakenly marked for a Monday delivery instead of Saturday. We've charged upwards of $20,000 on our personal American Express cards for one shoot and felt like we were going to be thrown in jail when the reimbursement hadn't come through. We've worked with celebrities who are complete disasters when it comes to dressing themselves. Somehow, those of us in this styling cabal can take it. It's just a part of the job.

With this book, I've channeled all of my experiences and knowledge about fashion, celebrity, gossip, and styling into one place. This is an in-depth look at the glamorous and gritty world of styling. *The Secrets of Stylists* is meant to help you—aspiring stylists and fashionistas—understand how much work lies ahead and how rewarding it is to focus on what you love.

In the following pages, you'll discover all you need to know to make it in this business. You'll hear from top stylists from across the globe, get tons of insider tips, examine celebrity looks (the good *and* the bad), and learn how to pull it all together at the most important moment. There is a dark side to all of this glamour, and it's important to know that up front. My success and longevity in this business have come from working for some of the worst people in the world but learning from the best. All of us stylists have done the grunt work: walking with garment bags on our shoulders through the snow, lugging scores of shopping bags back to Barneys and Saks, unpacking boxes with no help, and being on the receiving end of people screaming at us for not sending their cars on time to the airport. This is, I'm afraid, the only way to learn.

If you're like me, you want to work in fashion because you love it and you can't think of anything else you'd rather do. This guide will help you get started. Fasten your seat belts! It's going to be a fabulous ride.

CHAPTER ONE

Becoming a Stylist

Today, it seems like everyone wants to be a celebrity stylist. Before Uma Thurman showed up at the Oscars in Prada in 1995, the job description didn't even exist. But with the current onslaught of TV shows, movies, and YouTube videos portraying the lives of stylists, it's become one of the most sought-after careers. In fact, it's turned into a full-fledged business that can bring name recognition, a plethora of jobs, and a nice hefty paycheck. It's an amazing feeling to create a style, calling in gown no. 27 from a designer like Balenciaga and getting it on your girl, or launching a trend

and tidal wave of publicity for your client. But along with all the glamour comes some grit. In this chapter I'll break down for you the many pluses and a few minuses of this career calling.

THE GLAMOUR

Let's start with the glamorous side of styling. A great stylist delivers something unexpected: She or he changes a sleeve, nips the waist, or shortens the dress to make it fall better and show something never seen before. She or he uses a sharp eye to look at a table teeming with randomly placed scarves, picks one up, wraps it around a client's waist with a big gold or silver belt, and presto, a trend is born, copied, and manufactured! A top stylist has the luxury of being invited to fashion shows and seeing collections six months before anyone else and before the clothes hit department stores or boutique floors. A high-profile stylist may also have full entrée to work with a designer on made-to-order looks for his or her client.

By putting a celeb in a certain brand, a stylist can give a company worldwide exposure. Stylists have the power to move fashion along and allow it to evolve. Sahar Sanjar, president of laChambre, a Los Angeles–based public relations firm that represents designer Elie Saab, told me: "Celebrity stylists are so important. Without them, the brands that are up-and-coming or the brands that are trying to change their look will never get exposure. Celebrity dressing has changed so much. It's one thing to have a [magazine] editor behind the brand. But it's a totally different ballgame when you have a celebrity stylist support a brand."

Booth Moore, the fashion critic for the *Los Angeles Times,* told me: "As stylists have become celebrities in their own right, they've gotten a lot of exposure in magazines. It's looked upon as a glamorous job because a stylist is at the intersection of fashion and Hollywood—two very glamorous worlds. From the outside, it looks like stylists sit in the front

Uma Thurman, Academy Awards, Los Angeles, March 1995

Gwen Stefani with her stylist, Andrea Lieberman, Paris Fashion Week, March 2005

Kristen Davis, Sarah Jessica Parker, and stylist Patricia Field, Narciso Rodriguez at New York Fashion Week, September 2002

Christina Applegate with her stylist, Jessica Paster, New Year's Eve Party at Beso in Hollywood, December 31, 2008

Rihanna and her stylist, Mariel Haenn, at Jean-Paul Gaultier, Paris, October 3, 2009

row of fashion shows, go to swank parties, and get their pick of the world's best clothes. Most people don't see the drudgery behind the scenes: the hauling of clothes from place to place, waiting for clients, dealing with indecision, et cetera." This is the absolute truth. As gorgeous and glittery as everything is, there is a ton of really hard work to do.

Celebrity stylist Lee Harris added: "There seem to be several 'reality' shows based on stylists. I would say those shows depict very specific slices of heightened reality, so anyone expecting to work as a stylist—and party and go to fashion shows every day—is missing a huge reality of the business. So much of my time is spent researching on my computer, driving to appointments, and scouting stores for new looks." Yes, there is a menial side to the job.

THE GRIT

A typical day can start around 4:00 or 5:00 A.M. It usually entails some sort of high drama, likely over whether you'll ever receive the dress that you had set your heart on, ordered from a particular designer or showroom. There's a lot of getting on your knees, enduring a model who's

leaning on your head when you're fitting him or her in shoes, organizing racks of clothing, lining up heels in the right order, and taping the soles of fifty pairs of shoes so you can return them without having to pay the full retail price of $800 each.

The job may require you to unpack then repack dozens of trays of jewelry, only to unpack them then repack them yet again so they can be returned to their original owner in proper order. It's cleaning cups and making Starbucks runs. It's missing flights and best friends' birthday dinners. It's waiting for a package that's been erroneously shipped to another state. It's working for some of the most horrendous human beings on the planet. (Don't be surprised if you are called names, are spoken down to, have things thrown at your head, or never get credit for genius ideas that you came up with.)

Don't be dumbstruck when you're renamed "Midget," "Thing-y," or "Tranny" when something completely minor transpires that sets your client off. You will deal with egos the size of Cincinnati and be forced to endure ear-piercing tantrums. Call H.R.? Most likely there won't be any human resources to save you. Feel hurt and want to cry?

Q & A WITH STYLIST JESSICA PASTER

Jessica Paster may be best known to the public for the time she spent as Jessica Simpson's stylist as well as Christina Applegate, Hilary Duff, and Britney Spears, but she also paved the way for the styling business in Los Angeles. She's also well known for styling fashion icon Cate Blanchett and, most recently, Dakota Fanning.

WHAT'S A COMMON MISCONCEPTION ABOUT THE BUSINESS?

Young people think they're going to pick up the phone, get a rack of clothes, or better yet, they're going to pick one dress, and show the client one dress, and it's fine. When I prep for somebody, usually I would like two weeks for prepping, and we work our butts off. I have three girls right now doing FedEx shipping alone. I look at my door and I have one, two, three, four, five, six, seven, eight, nine, ten, eleven, twelve, thirteen, fourteen, fifteen, sixteen, seventeen, eighteen packages that are being sent out. My poor assistant comes in between six and seven, and she doesn't leave until nine o'clock. She walked in today, and I said, "What's wrong with you?" And she said, "I'm exhausted." I mean, this is a twenty-four-year-old who looks like she's hitting thirty.

Not all of us are lucky enough to be like the lovely Rachel Zoe and have somebody as amazing as Taylor Jacobson do all the work so she can look fabulous. We work. Last night I wanted to go to three parties: *GQ,* Katy Perry, and *Us Weekly.* Well, guess what? I worked until 9:30, and by the time I took a bath and sat down, my eyes couldn't stay open.

WHAT DO YOU LOVE ABOUT STYLING?

From the beginning, I loved that I was never a staunch fashionista—[those] who live and breathe fashion. I wasn't one of those weirdos who would die for a pair of, back then, Manolos. I didn't care about all of that. I still don't. But everything I own is from a major designer. I don't think I own a cheap pair of shoes or a cheap garment. I've always been very chic and clean, never outrageous. I also think that timing was a very important factor in my career. To be honest with you, if I started now to be a stylist, I wouldn't be able to.

WHY IS THAT?

First of all, it's now a full business. Styling wasn't as mainstream as it is right now. Back then, when I called Alexander McQueen, I'd say, "I want this look." The next day, I got the dress. Now you have to send an e-mail two weeks before, and if they don't think it's for Charlize Theron, they won't send it to you.

Now designers have hired P.R. people who think they know about fashion. They're a joke. This whole business is a joke, to be honest with you. Yesterday I did a shoot where I was literally on my hands and knees buckling the bottom of a Cavalli bathing suit to an actress. Do you know how many times I've gotten on my hands and knees and applied lotion because their bunions are so big? I've done it without thinking about ego. It's a different ball of wax right now. When I started, you had Lori Goldstein and Arianne Phillips. Now there are a whole a bunch of people styling. And I get outbid because somebody will do a job for nothing. For instance, my agent got this "20th Century Fox has a no stylist fee policy" [memo]. One of my longtime clients is Christina Applegate. I said, "Well, you have to tell Ms. Applegate that if she would like me to dress her, and I've dressed her forever, I would love to dress her but I'm not going to dress her for free." Three days later, my agent said, "We got you money." And I'm supposed to say thank you for paying me for my job. It wasn't like that back then. People valued our talent. Now, everyone's a stylist.

WHAT INFLUENCES YOU? WHAT DO YOU LOVE?

What I love about my job is when you get someone like Dakota Fanning, put her in a beautiful Valentino gown, and she gets it. When she walks the red carpet you see that you've done something special. All the stars are aligned. I love that.

WHAT INSPIRES YOU IN EACH JOB?

I like to do my homework. I have books upon books upon books, and I'm an old movie buff—I love everything Old Hollywood. I always try to bring a little bit of that history into each of my jobs.

WHAT IS YOUR BEST STYLING SECRET?

Undergarments, such as things to make your boobies look good, things to make your tummy flatter, and things to make your waist smaller. For instance, I can take three inches away from someone's waist.

WHOM WOULD YOU LOVE TO STYLE, DEAD OR ALIVE?

I would have loved to work with Marilyn Monroe. I think I would have made an impact on her wardrobe as well as on her life. And then I would have loved to work with Ava Gardner because she so reminds me of me. Also Hedy Lamarr because, to this day, I don't think there's ever been a more beautiful woman. And alive, the two women I would love to work with are Jessica Lange and Meryl Streep.

WHAT KIND OF IMPACT DO YOU THINK STYLING CAN HAVE ON A STAR?

You can make someone's fashion career. Cate Blanchett did not become Cate Blanchett by herself. I did Cate Blanchett for nine years. She was on every best-dressed list.

WHAT KIND OF IMPACT DO YOU THINK STYLING HAS ON REGULAR WOMEN?

Talking about the First Lady, sales went up for the Gap and for J.Crew when she wore their sweaters. She took a designer, Jason Wu, and made him a household name. You put a certain purse on a certain woman, say Nicole Kidman, and everybody who aspires to be her or loves her will go out and buy this purse. So fashion on a celebrity makes a huge impact.

IF YOU WERE TO MENTOR SOMEONE WHO'S JUST STARTING OUT, WHAT WOULD YOUR WORDS OF WISDOM BE?

Always follow your heart and your dreams. If you really, really want to be a stylist, please pursue it. Know that it's less glamorous than you think. Know that you're giving up a lot of your life to do this, because it's not about picking one dress. I work nothing less than ten-hour days. I've chosen to sacrifice much of my life because it's something that I love. But know that you really, really need to work hard.

Angie Harmon, Michelle Monaghan, Jamie Tisch, stylist Mary Alice Stephenson, and Kerry Washington at Kara Ross Oscar Collection party at Sunset Tower Hotel, Los Angeles, February 21, 2008

Vanessa Hudgens with stylist Deborah Waknin, Movieline's Hollywood Lifestyle Awards, Los Angeles, October 7, 2007

Public relations maven Kelly Cutrone infamously said, "If you have to cry, go outside," which is also the title of her popular book. Because no one really cares at the end of the day if you're insulted, unhappy, or your feelings are hurt.

You will face seemingly endless rounds of fashion shows or appointments with designers; fine-jewelry runs; call-ins for suits, dresses, gowns, jeans, and shoes; conference calls with studios, agents, and P.R. folk; conversations with the "glam squad" (hair, nail, and makeup masters); researching and editing looks; and run-throughs with dresses. And this is all in the span of just one day.

That said, once all the dirty work is done, and your client is styled for his or her red carpet moment or you "get the shot," you'll get the ultra-satisfaction of seeing your vision realized. That's what makes it all worthwhile.

TYPES OF STYLISTS

There are many different classes of stylists and styling gigs. How do you know which of the wide array is for you? Here's a short list of the different types:

CELEBRITY STYLIST

The big-daddy, high-profile celebrity stylist finds gowns for red carpet events and clothing for movie press junkets and personal appearances. She or he essentially oversees the full look and collaborates with the glam squad—hair, makeup, and nail stylists. This stylist can juggle up to five or more clients for an awards show with a team of assistants

Q & A WITH LORI GOLDSTEIN

Lori Goldstein is one of the most sought-after editorial stylists in the fashion industry. She's worked on Madonna videos and Versace ad campaigns and with every photographer and hip publication you can think of. She's also inspired a lot of today's top L.A. stylists.

HOW IS WHAT YOU DO DIFFERENT FROM PERSONAL STYLING?

As I'm doing QVC and starting to come out from behind the scenes, the term *celebrity stylist* always comes up. But I'm not a celebrity stylist. The difference is that I work with celebrities on particular jobs—for magazines more than anything else—not for their personal lives. I'm hired by magazines or photographers. For instance, I just did Rihanna for *W*, and they asked, "Would you do her video?" I also just did Daniel Day-Lewis and Penélope Cruz for the *New York Times.*

I've only styled two people in my career personally. One was Demi Moore years ago. We just met, and I got along with her and became friends with her personal assistant. It was fun. I had a credit card and I would go to Barneys and shop like I would for myself, and then go play dress-up at her house. Same with Madonna.

TELL ME ABOUT YOUR COLLABORATIVE PROCESS WHEN YOU'RE DEALING WITH AN EDITORIAL SHOOT.

I believe in the team and everybody who's involved, from the art director to the photographer. We all talk about what our needs are, what needs to get done, who we're shooting, where we want to take it, and how we want him or her to look. A lot of times, especially with a celebrity, you don't get to meet them beforehand.

And then there's working with the designer, which I love. I worked with Donatella for five years. I'm not a Versace girl, but I totally got who she was and understood the needs of that company, which now we would call a brand, but we didn't then. I love working with Carolina Herrera—I'm so not a Herrera woman, but I love her and love getting into the whole head of that world. Vera's been amazing too.

WHAT IS YOUR SECRET STYLING WEAPON?

My weapon is that I'm fearless. I just go for it. You really can't make a mistake in fashion. You keep looking and trying. It's like a painting you're creating, and all of a sudden you see, you've got it.

HOW IMPORTANT IS IT TO KNOW ABOUT DRAPE, CUT, FIT, AND TAILORING?

It's so important. The more you know, the better you're going to be at your job. I've had assistants ask, "What's a houndstooth?" Or "What's a bias?" Not that you're going to know all of this in the beginning, but the more you know, the better you'll do.

who sometimes get to work hands on with a celebrity. A celebrity stylist has a strong sense of her client, knows the market, can direct fashion photo shoots, has an excellent track record and reputation, and is a great boss to aspiring stylists. Now, what will you be paid? A premier celebrity stylist can make anywhere between $1,500 and $5,000 per day but could also command $5,000 to $20,000 a day—it all depends on who the client is. With the recession, everything has come down. Also, this fee comes directly from the studio when the job is attached to a film. Celebrities who go out to an event that's not attached to a film sometimes get the styling as a favor by the stylist.

FASHION EDITORIAL STYLIST

This type of stylist usually works on staff at a major fashion monthly or weekly glossy. He or she works with a team of coworkers and reports directly to the editor in chief of the magazine. The job requires overseeing all photo shoots—both fashion and beauty—that come to the magazine, as well as overseeing a department. It entails booking photographers, glam squads, and models or celebrities, plus arranging props, locations, and travel. Editorial stylists are also responsible for working on setting up photo shoots, directing them, and laying them out. They are also in touch with the "advertising side," which handles all of the fashion advertising that comes in (and pays the bills). Editorial stylists have a vast knowledge of the clothing and the players and shoot on a monthly or weekly basis. What can you expect to get paid? This is tricky. If you're a junior editor or stylist you can make approximately $25k plus overtime: $35k to $40k a year. Expenses are usually picked up by, or billed directly to, the magazine you work for. If you've already worked at another publication, you can make more, but everyone's salary is completely different. Freelance magazine jobs are approximately $250 for prep day; $250 for day of shoot; $250 to return everything after the shoot.

ADVERTISING STYLIST

The job of an advertising stylist is almost the same as an editorial stylist, except that you're typically an independent contractor (or sometimes on staff at a major publication). You get hired in one of two ways: it's a lot of who you know, and if an agency is booking a stylist, it's through their calling in your portfolio and looking at your work. This job involves all the same duties as a fashion editorial stylist, but usually with a larger budget. This pay scale can go from $800 to $3,500 a day.

PERSONAL STYLIST

A personal stylist works with individual clients, including celebrities who aren't necessarily walking the red carpet all the time, television newscasters, other on-air personalities, and women who just need to have their looks put together. Personal stylists find clothes for their clients' appearances and special occasions. They know a great deal about style and fashion, along with how to tailor clothes and adorn the body. You can expect rates between $1,500 and $4,000 per day for a celebrity and approximately $100 a day for real women who are looking for help with styling.

WARDROBE STYLIST

Styling a wardrobe involves updating a private client's personal closet. A wardrobe stylist helps the client decide what to keep and what to dump, editing out pieces that are too old, don't fit, or don't suit the personality of the client. There's a personal-shopping aspect to this job, whereby the stylist buys a wardrobe and delivers it to the client's house. A wardrobe stylist earns around $50 an hour.

MY DEVIL WORE YSL

MY FIRST BOSS WAS A DEVIL. I started out as a below-junior-level assistant at *Vanity Fair*, working for this Amazonian woman from Italy named Marina Schiano. And she wore Yves Saint Laurent. She scared the crap out of me. Seriously. I was always in fear that I was going to get my ass fired, even if I did good work. Looking back now, I see that I got a lot from this sort of training, as did her other assistants. It kept us from acting entitled or like know-it-alls. Well, occasionally I did act like an idiot, but I was young and stupid, and ultimately I learned fast. The devil would yell at me in all different languages, even when she was in a good mood. So I never really could sit back and relax, which is another good thing. There was absolutely nothing touchy-feely between us.

After an incident involving smashed dog biscuits we delivered to fashion designer Carolina Herrera's office as a Christmas gift, we parted ways. Even though I apologized profusely for the crumbled dog food,

PERSONAL SHOPPER

A personal shopping specialist works at a department store or online, offering advice on what's current and modern and what type of clothing, color, and silhouette is ideal for a specific client. Often hired to create looks for various trips, events, or special occasions, this stylist must have a vast awareness of designers in both clothing and accessories to create a complete head-to-toe look and wardrobe. The personal shopper's fee starts at approximately $500 a day and goes up from there.

TELEVISION WARDROBE STYLIST

Reporters, news anchors, and weather forecasters hire stylists to advise them on how to dress for their day-to-day on-air appearances as well as for events. More and more on-air personalities are outing their stylists in webisodes, during which they discuss how their stylist chose an outfit for a particular event. This sort of job can eventually lead to a personal styling gig as you network and grow your relationships with other people at the TV network. Pay varies depending on the job and whether or not the show is union. If the show is union, the scale starts at approximately $28 an hour. (With union TV, depending on whether a celebrity brings you in, you can negotiate your hourly rate, which can be significantly higher than union scale.) If it's a non-union show, the stylist works on a flat day-rate ranging anywhere from $150 to thousands of dollars a day, depending on the type of show and the experience level of the stylist.

ASSISTANT STYLIST

An entry-level assistant job usually entails setting up racks and calling in and returning samples of clothing, accessories, and shoes from showrooms and stores. Steaming, taping, wiring, and gluing are all tasks you'll learn how to do on the job. You can end up assisting a stylist on a red carpet assignment or manning the phones at the office. In the beginning, you may have to work free, though the "pay" comes in experience and sometimes cool threads. Some assistant stylists get an hourly wage or day rate. The rates depend on how much the lead stylist rakes in for a job, which can translate to take-home averages of $150 to $300 per day.

BORN TO STYLE

A stylist is only as good as his or her last look. Stylists who ultimately make it have worked long hours, for deplorable people, and in deplorable conditions and have given up most of their personal free time to do what they really, truly love. They have paid their dues and some. These are people who are very smart, who have amazing eyes for spotting what's going to make a meteoric impact and set trends. They have extremely loyal clients, do not "dress and tell," and are most content staying behind the scenes, very rarely wanting to be seen or, God forbid, appear in print.

The one thing I find really amazing is that once they're in it, no one speaks of getting out. They all know they were born to do this. There are days that are dreadful, but they never say they want out. There's a desire to be around the drama, the intensity, and the clothing. It's a lot of hard work, but it pays off because you're doing something you have a passion for. The greatest thing about fashion and style is that it constantly changes and evolves. There's never a dull moment. There's always something going on: a new awards show, a fresh fashion week with a new season with different clothing and ideas. Think about it: what's not to love?

---

it didn't work—I didn't know how to keep it together, shut up, and just take the tongue lashing. I never had any intention of taking over her job (though I may have fantasized about gently pushing her down a flight of stairs à la *Showgirls*), but I should have let my young ambition take a backseat so that I could continue working with and learning from Marina.

Even though that job ended badly, I knew I wanted to stick with styling and fashion because I was so damn passionate about it. I loved the fact that clothing came and went on a somewhat hourly basis. I loved the drama and the Sturm und Drang when I tried to yank a dress off another magazine's rack for an actress like Jessica Lange or Michelle Pfeiffer. And even when my spirit was down, I decided I was going to do this come hell or high water, behind the scenes or not. I stuck to it and here I am, twenty-plus years later.

CHAPTER TWO

What It Takes

So you think you have what it takes to be a great stylist? Ready to persevere through a lot of grueling, menial tasks for a while? Willing to prove yourself with that positive attitude? Well, let's find out. In this chapter you'll hear from other paragons in the industry; through their own words, you'll get a sense of the learning curve. You'll also learn ten ways to hone your styling sensibility, how to land a job, and, most important, how to keep your job while remaining sane and in good standing with your boss and everyone else. There's a lot of work ahead. Are you ready?

GETTING YOUR FOOT IN THE DOOR

Like many creative jobs, no manual exists for styling. And there's no blueprint for how to break in to the business. Before you can get your foot in the door, you need to know which doors to knock on. Should you send out a bevy of e-mails or make phone calls? And to whom? Do you resort to a Gorilla Gram to make your voice heard?

Deborah Waknin, the Hollywood styling pioneer whose clients include Halle Berry, Sandra Bullock, and Vanessa Hudgens, had this to say about her beginnings: "I was studying in New York to become a theater costume designer. Before I finished school, I worked with commercial stylists. I did it completely for free. I was the assistant who schlepped." Read more about Waknin in her interview on page 28.

Here's how a few other stylist/designers and stylists broke into the biz, in their own words:

Barbara Tfank *(illustration, left), fashion designer who famously dressed Uma Thurman for the 1995 Oscars in Prada, ushering in the era of high-end designers on the red carpet:*

"I was a design assistant in Richard Avedon's studio in the '80s. I was the junior, junior person. I started as the assistant to the stylist, and then I went on to do a couple of things for *Self* magazine. Avedon used to show me all of his pictures from *Harper's Bazaar*, which inspired me."

Nicole Chavez, *stylist for and close friend of Rachel Bilson and Kristen Bell:*

"I studied art and design with a focus on photography in college. I really enjoyed the prepping aspects: casting my models, styling the shoots, and conceptualizing it. After

Uma Thurman, Prada Sketch

Rachel Zoe adjusts Jessica Simpson's dress at "Divas" Benefit for Save the Music Foundation, MGM Grand Hotel, Las Vegas, April 18, 2004.

Q & A WITH PENNY LOVELL

Stylist Penny Lovell has worked in London, New York, and Los Angeles. Her best-known client is fashion industry darling Ginnifer Goodwin.

HOW DID YOU BUILD YOUR CLIENT BASE?

When I started, I met my clients at photo shoots, but these days they usually get referred to me.

WHO HAVE YOU ASSISTED IN THE PAST?

I used to assist a fashion editor at British *Elle*, then the fashion director of the *Sunday Telegraph* magazine in the U.K.

DO YOU ACTUALLY DRESS CLIENTS OR DO YOU LET YOUR ASSISTANT DO IT?

I like to dress clients myself, but the support from my assistant is also essential. It frees me up to just think about the look and not worry about logistics.

WHO DO YOU THINK HAS THE BEST PERSONAL STYLE?

So many people have great style. I am a fan of people who are true to themselves and are consistent, who look confident and happy, which is the most important thing regardless of what they are wearing. Outside of my clients—obviously!—I'd say Diane Kruger, Julianne Moore, Marion Cotillard, Anna Wintour, and Alexa Chung.

WHAT IS THE MOST VALUABLE LESSON YOU'VE LEARNED?

The most valuable lesson I learned was from Kim Hunt, whom I assisted for three years. She taught me to listen, trust my instincts, stay calm, and be flexible. You don't have to be in a very expensive well-known-designer dress to look stylish. A couple of years ago, a dress of Ginnifer's was listed as one the years best in *Harper's Bazaar* and it cost $8 at a flea market.

DO YOU EVER BRING AN EMERGENCY KIT ON THE CARPET?

I do take a mini kit with me on the carpet. In fact, in my wallet I permanently carry a mini sewing kit, double-sided tape, and Band-Aids!

WHAT'S IN YOUR PERSONAL STYLING WARDROBE?

I mainly wear black clothes and always flats to work! Ease and comfort first! Although luckily with the privileges that this job gives you—discounts, et cetera—I do have a good wardrobe to choose from. For events, obviously I dress appropriately for the occasion, so I bust out some heels for that!

WHAT'S YOUR BEST ADVICE TO AN ASPIRING STYLIST?

Always remember this is a business, it's not dress-up. Professionalism is key. Assist, listen and learn, and get to know the business and how it works. It's not just about creating looks. You do a tremendous amount of dealing with people—clients, designers, publicists, managers, magazines, photographers, et cetera—so you need great people skills. It's the most important thing I look for in an assistant. Plus, long-term persistence really pays off. So many people want to get involved in this industry but it seems to me only the ones who really get stuck in for the long haul succeed.

I graduated in '98, I worked for an interior designer who asked me, "What do you want to be?" And I said, "I love fashion. I want to be a costume designer. I want to be around clothing and work in the business." So he called his friend who was the head of production at Disney, and she said, "If you can fly yourself out here, if you can put yourself up for the whole time of the shoot, we'll hire you as a local production assistant in the wardrobe department, and you can get your feet wet." So I did—and fell in love with the process. She got me a job as a P.A. to be an extra pair of hands on a movie set. The wardrobe department took me in and taught me a lot. I left that experience wanting more, so when I came back to L.A., the friends I had met working on the movie helped me get into the next movie and the union."

Lee Harris, stylist responsible for the many glorious red carpet looks of Drew Barrymore and Lucy Liu:

"I got started as a set costumer and shopper for films and television shows. It was an invaluable experience, because I challenged myself to learn as much as possible about period clothing and dressing characters. I got the chance to dress hundreds of great actors with vastly different body types and learned how different silhouettes and fabrics work on an extremely wide range of shapes."

Penny Lovell, stylist for Rose Byrne and Ginnifer Goodwin:

"I was working at a P.R. agency in London, where I met fashion editors and stylists. I decided to leave [the agency] to assist them as a freelancer. I worked really hard and 'did my time.' I assisted for almost four years because I always felt it was important to learn everything I could before I moved on to the next stage and not let early ambition ruin what I wanted to be a long career. I started in fashion and eventually moved on to dressing actors."

Tara Swennen, stylist for young Hollywood stars, including Kristen Stewart, Lauren Conrad, Miley Cyrus, and Paula Patton:

"I started out as an intern at Barneys New York in its studio services department [a special area of the store where experts help stylists and costumers select wardrobe and props for shoots, soap operas, and sitcoms]. My first day on the job I met a number of stylists and costume designers, including Andrea Lieberman. Although I had aspirations of becoming a clothing designer, I was intrigued by this new twist on the profession. Styling allowed me to make a plethora of looks without having to go through the lengthy and complicated construction and manufacturing process. I realized I could have the best of both worlds."

Cristina Ehrlich, stylist who retooled Nicole Richie's image and famously dressed Penélope Cruz for the 2009 Oscars in a vintage Balmain dress:

"Since I was young, my two obsessions have been dance and fashion. I was a professional dancer until I was twenty-seven, and when I decided to retire from dance, fashion and styling was the obvious next step. I started assisting stylists in Los Angeles on any job I could find—commercials, photo shoots—and worked my way up. The years I spent as a dancer were incredibly helpful for this business. Having spent many hours at the ballet barre perfecting body lines gave me a deeper appreciation of how fabrics, silhouettes, and draping accentuate the female form."

Phillip Bloch, the "fashion yenta" and überstylist who's worked with everyone from Salma Hayek to Nicole Kidman to Jada Pinkett Smith and is the author of The Shopping Diet:

"I was in NYC doing commercials and editorial in the early '90s, but my goal was to work with recording artists in L.A. I knew there were plenty of stylists in Hollywood, but they didn't have any New York connections, so I went out there. A year or two after Uma Thurman wore the lavender Prada dress to the Oscars, things took off and I dressed about eleven people for the Academy Awards."

BASIC TRAINING

Because there's no formal training program for styling, you'll need to educate yourself. Take every opportunity you can to build your portfolio and résumé. Here are some steps to take to get the experience you'll need:

1. DEVOTE YOURSELF TO YOUR DREAM

Styling may not be as important as curing cancer, but I believe that dressing someone can make a powerful statement and say a lot about who your client is. So nurture your passion and stand by your vision. You'll need the courage of your convictions and dedication. The styling world is freakishly competitive, so you must be able to take rejection and handle stress without letting go of your dream.

2. STUDY, STUDY, STUDY

Make it your business to read fashion magazines of all sorts, devouring the direction and the ideas in the pictures. Tear out the pages and keep what you like in notebooks or organizers. Refer back to them for inspiration when it's time to put together an idea or look. Use them as visuals to illustrate your concept when collaborating with a team.

Q & A WITH DEBORAH WAKNIN

Another of L.A.'s most sought-after stylists, Deborah Waknin is probably best known for her work with Halle Berry and Sandra Bullock. She almost never misses on the red carpet.

WHAT IS A KEY PIECE OF ADVICE YOU WOULD GIVE TO FLEDGLING STYLISTS?

You have to be extremely honest and extremely respectful of the clothes. If you say you're going to return something on a certain date, you make sure that it goes back in better shape than the way you received it. It's really, really key. If the garment is dirty, get it dry-cleaned. Wrap it up in tissue.

Designers will loan me anything because I'm so strict about paperwork and having it in impeccable order. I'm so OCD that, believe it or not, I do everything in alphabetical order. The shoes and clothes are all in alphabetical order by designer. That's the system that works for me, and everyone knows where everything is. The other thing that I tell most of the girls is to be smart when the looks come in. Immediately check the paperwork and make sure that what you pulled is actually in the bag.

WHY DO YOU THINK STYLING HAS BECOME SO IMPORTANT?

Quite honestly, anything that a celebrity wears, because they're borrowing clothes, indirectly garners press for whatever designer loaned it. It creates a huge amount of buzz and money for the designers. So I think now they're more willing to lend.

HAVE YOU EVER WANTED TO WALK THE CARPET?

Nope. Never wanted to be on TV. Never want a reality show. Phillip Bloch was the person who wanted to do that, and now it's Rachel and a few others. Mind you, they get paid very well, but that's what they want. I want to do fabulous work whereby people within the industry know who I am. And that gives me time to be a family person. I have my child, I have my lifestyle, we take off the month of August, and we go away for Christmas.

TELL ME ABOUT YOUR COLLABORATIVE PROCESS.

I am that stylist who collaborates. It's imperative. For me, my client is like a director. They say, "This is the event, this is where I'm at in my life, and I would very much like to find things that work within that lifestyle." And I take that into consideration, along with the colors that they like, the shapes that they like, and where their body's at. I go on Style.com, go through all my lookbooks, and do an entire book from A to Z of colored images of certain dresses that I think would be appropriate for their events. Then I send it to my client and they earmark it. And then at that point, I call the designers and I see if they're available or if they're interested in sending out for certain events. I've done it for everyone I work with: Leslie Mann, Sandra Bullock, Halle [Berry], Vanessa [Hudgens], Miley Cyrus. It makes it really nice for them to see where my mind is in terms of what I want to do with them.

My best moment was the 2009 Oscars with both Vanessa and Halle, when I literally hounded Marchesa to get me these two dresses, which were then stuck in customs up until three days before the event. We had other options, and they were phenomenal, and we had them ready. You should always have your first choice and then your second first choice because on the day, you don't know where the body is going to be, how comfortable they're going to be in the dress they chose.

WHAT'S YOUR GREAT INSIDE STYLING SECRET?

Make sure the client is comfortable: that the shoes are comfortable, and that she's comfortable in the dress. That's it.

Read the credits on the pages and remember the names of the stylists whose work you admire; search online for their résumés to see whom else they've been responsible for styling. (FashionCopius.typepad.com is a great resource to download tons of European editorials as well as American ones.)

Start to learn designers' names. J. Logan Horne, who has worked with Hayden Panettiere and Leighton Meester, told me this knowledge is key when an aspiring assistant wants to make a great impression. When interviewing, Horne looks for "someone who knows what they are talking about and is thinking ahead of fashion. If I ask someone who their favorite designer is and they say 'Chanel,' the meeting goes no further. Now, if they say Karl Lagerfeld, then we can talk."

Take note: Even though Coco Chanel (1883–1971) may be remembered as the greatest designer of the twentieth century, Karl Lagerfeld has been at the helm of the company since 1983, when he became design director. So when you refer to these names—Dior (John Galliano), YSL (Stefano Pilati), Fendi (also Lagerfeld), Lanvin (Alber Elbaz), and Calvin Klein (Francisco Costa)—know their origins and design directors!

And one more thing: Don't make the mistake of mispronouncing designers' names. You'll look like a total rookie.

3. MAKE THE INTERNET YOUR BEST FRIEND

Ideally, you'd attend fashion shows to see how clothing moves on the body and how looks are put together. But if you aren't able to go just yet, you can view fashion shows on Style.com, Nytimes.com, and Nymag.com. You can also search the Web sites' archives for new and old looks. In addition to runway Web sites, there are many blogs and sites devoted to stylists, designers, and what celebrities wear and where they shop. These sites have become an integral part of the industry landscape. See the Resources section at the end of this book for a guide to my favorite fashion Web sites.

4. CHOOSE A FOCUS

There are a handful of jobs that can be stepping stones to getting you closer to being a celebrity stylist (see Types of Stylists, page 20). These more junior positions can put you in contact with a celebrity who may need assistance dressing for an awards show or red carpet event. They can also help you to meet a mentor—someone you can bounce ideas off and who can teach you about drape, fit, and tailoring. No matter which focus you choose, you will be around clothing. And the more you work on putting together outfits

and developing a sense of your client's requirements, the sharper your eye will become for choosing great looks, style, and textures.

5. PUT YOURSELF IN THEIR SHOES

Yes, try on shoes from Jimmy Choo, YSL, Christian Louboutin, Stuart Weitzman (below), Fendi, and Giuseppe Zanotti. It's impossible to know what it's like to walk in those shoes unless you've done it. Learn about heel heights (Manolo Blahnik has many height versions of the same fabulous pointed-toe pumps and sling backs) and types, such as platforms, sling backs, d'Orsays, et cetera. Make shoe salespeople your best friends so that they can train you on what's hot, what's selling, and who's making the best for the season. And get on those waiting lists to get the shoes for your client first.

6. ESTABLISH A PERSONAL POINT OF VIEW—A MISSION STATEMENT OF SORTS

Write down what inspires you, whose style changed your life, and whose philosophy you believe in. Whose looks do you love? Phillip Bloch's Halle Barry when she won an Oscar? Eric Daman's crazy-sexy-cool for the *Gossip Girls* on television? June Ambrose's tailored and classic chic-ghetto-fab with an edge? Patricia Field's Carrie, Samantha, Charlotte, or Miranda? Rachel Zoe's California cool?

Study celebrities you like and reference Web sites like CelebrityStyleguide.com to see the designers the celebrities are wearing. Tear out ads and magazine editorials. Organize the visuals by style, model, and date, or collage them on a wall or bulletin board in a way that's pleasing to your eye.

7. BE YOUR OWN MUSE

Try on clothes to see how designers cut their pieces. What makes a jacket from Chanel work, and how does it compare to a younger, boxier cut from Marc Jacobs? Try it on, study the weight of the jacket, how it fits, and where it hits the body. Why does the John Galliano bias-cut dress fit almost every body? Check out his Dior gowns as well. Find out why celebrities and stylists always request James Perse long-sleeve V-neck T-shirts. Look into who makes the best pants for all bodies.

Paul Cavaco, creative director of *Allure,* told me that the best designer pants to fit all bodies are made by Sonia Rykiel. My pick? Express's luxury stretch Editor Pant. For the best basics, stylist J. Logan Horne suggests the Row, the line created by Mary-Kate and Ashley Olsen. He says Proenza Schouler cuts the most amazing jackets. Try it all on and get a feel for what you're putting your potential clients in.

8. BUILD YOUR RÉSUMÉ

Take an internship or assistant position. Assisting a "veteran" in the business at a fashion magazine will give you a chance to see how looks are put together. Train with someone who has a strong sense of reference, and pay attention. Even if a magazine isn't your ideal workplace, it's a great place to start. Or work as a wardrobe assistant on television shows, movies, newscasts, reality TV, and entertainment shows so that you can network and get referred to additional jobs.

9. BUILD A PORTFOLIO AND REFERENCES

You will need to show a potential client what you've done in the past. You'll need to show him or her your work, whether it's tear sheets from a photo shoot you've created or a reference from someone with whom you've worked for at least two years.

10. NETWORK

Because there isn't a school or formal training program for styling, you'll need to rely on yourself to get connected with people in the industry. Meet, greet, and speak to boutique owners, make friends with people in the record business, et cetera. Seriously think about all the people you've ever met and comb through how they can help you and arrange introductions. Social networking on services like Facebook and Twitter are key to making new friends and keeping the old ones informed about what you're doing. The more you talk to people, the more you'll find inroads to musicians, actresses, actors, television anchors, and TV hosts who need help dressing for events or tours.

Remember the list of stylists you compiled in step 6? Study it. Think about everyone you know who might have even the tiniest lead. Knock on doors, make phone calls, send out résumés, and read blogs like Fashionista.com.

Try linking up to an agency that has a stellar reputation and works with a nice stable of stylists. Make it your mission to know who all the key players are, from MMA (Margaret Maldonado Agency) to the Magnet to the Wall Group. Check their Web sites to see whom they represent, what type of work they specialize in, and who's hiring. Check the stylists' online portfolios, call the agents listed, and spell out your intentions.

Take note: It's not worth aligning yourself with a publicist who styles stars. Some stars use their publicists as stylists. The problem is that publicists really aren't trained. They know nothing about fit and tailoring. It's simply not something they do. In my experience, an unusually bad fit on a celebrity ultimately suggests the publicist did the styling. It's a cost-cutting move celebrities may undertake when a studio or movie is not paying for appearances. You may think that if you team up with a publicist who needs assistance shopping for the star, you'll get a foot in the door. Unfortunately, this is not the case.

GETTING—AND KEEPING—THE JOB

As I've said before, to make it in this business you have to start at the bottom and pay your dues. Look for an assistant or apprenticeship program first. You'll need at least two solid years of assisting to get enough experience to break out on your own. Sound like jail? It's a necessity. You have got to sell yourself, because if you wait around for someone to give you a job, you'll be on hold forever.

THE INTERVIEW

Employers are always looking for people who can go that extra step, who are "proactive problem solvers." Tara Swennen, who has many celebrity clients, told me: "The job is fast paced and hectic at times. I need people who remain calm under pressure and can come up with innovative solutions quickly while maintaining a positive attitude. No one wants to work with a grumpy stylist, so everyone on the team needs to be a pleasure to be around, no matter how stressful the situation. I also look for people of character. My assistants are like my family, and since we spend so much time together, who they are as people outside the job is of great importance to me. And of course, they have to love and adore fashion." God, wish I had trained with her first!

Q & A WITH LEE HARRIS

Lee has styled Drew Barrymore and Lucy Liu. He started as a set costumer and shopper for films and television, where he challenged himself to learn as much as possible about period clothing and dressing characters with different body types. He met Ms. Liu when working as a set costumer on Ally McBeal.

WHAT ADVICE DO YOU HAVE FOR SOMEONE LOOKING TO GET STARTED IN THE BUSINESS?

Be a great assistant for several years and learn everything you can about the business. The most successful stylists have put in their time and nurtured their businesses. Educate yourself about period clothing. Learn about fabrics and how they function in different garments. Learn about tailoring so you can pin a garment for alterations. Learn where every resource in your city is located: fabric stores, dry cleaners, tailors, shoe repairers, dyers. Always treat people with respect because you will run across the same names for your entire career.

Do not lie to get what you want. This is a global business but a rather small world. If you say you are pulling dresses for one client when you are really secretly pulling for someone else, people will find out. A shady reputation is very hard to escape.

WHAT MAKES A GREAT ASSISTANT?

My ideal assistant is discreet, loyal, knowledgeable about all the aspects of fashion and tailoring, quick, pleasant, familiar with all the local resources and shops, and, most important, someone who represents me with class and professionalism.

WHAT MISCONCEPTIONS DO PEOPLE HAVE ABOUT STYLING?

While there are many benefits, such as traveling and working with beautiful clothes, the hours can be incredibly long, and often ideas change at the last minute. It is my job to fulfill the new vision.

WHAT'S YOUR FAVORITE PART OF THE BUSINESS?

My favorite part of the celebrity styling business is the long-term relationships that I have developed with both actresses and designers. I've worked with my main clients for years, and it has been incredibly fulfilling for me to usher them through fashion transformations and to help them explore new styles.

ANY FAVORITE LOOKS YOU'VE STYLED?

My first globally photographed look was probably the Lucy Liu turquoise Versace gown. It was received very well by the press. A successful look gives me more of an internal satisfaction, as well as a shared joy between my client and me.

Lucy has had some amazing moments on the red carpet wearing Giambattista Valli—the custom-made red bubble dress she wore to the *Kung Fu Panda* premiere in London and the cream sheath and floral capelet that she wore to an Oscar party in 2008.

I am also extremely sentimental about all of the great moments that Drew [Barrymore] has had on the red carpet wearing Christian Dior: the pale blue couture gown at the 2009 Golden Globes, the pale pink chiffon couture gown at the 2007 Golden Globes, the acid green party dress at the NYC premiere for *Lucky You*. Additionally, I am proud of the work that Drew and I did for her *Grey Gardens* press tour, especially the pale peach beaded Alberta Ferretti gown and the headpiece for the NYC premiere. We were really trying to reach a happy medium of vintage flair with a modern sensibility, and I think we achieved our goal.

Swennen continued: "My biggest turnoff when looking at the new kids trying to break in to the business is laziness and an attitude of entitlement. I worked my ass off to get where I am today. And it seems like so many of this new crop of kids aren't interested in doing that. Being successful at anything takes hard work and years of dedication. That's never going to change. Many of the [aspiring stylists] I interview seem to think the job is nine-to-five and nothing more than running to Beverly Hills to shop. To do the job right, you have to be willing to put in long hours and get down and dirty. It's an art, and you have to devote yourself to it. I can't tell you the number of people I don't hire simply because their attitude walks in the door five feet in front of them."

A word to the wise: Be humble and learn everything you can from your boss. If you're giving off the air that you're above this or that, you'll be shown the door.

Interviewing Tips

When you go on an interview there are some obvious things you need to know:

①   Arrive early! Literally "audition" your look the night before you go to an interview so you know what you're going to wear ahead of time. You won't risk being late because you couldn't decide between the Miu Miu or the Manolo.

___

②   Research where you're headed. Prepare yourself. Google and read up on what's going to be asked of you in general terms, and think about what you want to ask: details about the job, what it entails, hours, how many others are on the team. You want it, go for it!

___

③   Work on a solid handshake. Seriously. The limp-fish hand turns me off immediately.

___

④   Obviously, you should look presentable. Your appearance gives the first impression. No matter how groovy and cool you are, make sure you look the part and mean business. Dress for the job you want and use common sense. If you're thinking the sequin hot pants with a cool, shlumpy white shirt is semi questionable then just forget it. If the skirt feels too short, it probably is. If it's a silk fabric and you think you'll "schvitz" (perspire) during the interview, wear cotton instead. If you're going into a corporate structure like Revlon or CNN, it's very important to dress the part. Get some pieces from J. Crew and then throw in some stylish, original accessories to make the look your own. If

you're interviewing at a magazine, you can certainly dress creatively, but keep in mind that it's still a corporate environment. You'll likely meet salespeople and managing editors who may or may not get your look. If you're going on a one-on-one interview at a house or an independent styling office, go ahead and show your true colors, but do not go overboard like Barbara Stanwyck did in *Stella Dallas* (Yep! Look that up!)

___

⑤   Body language 101: Do not swing your feet or legs, slouch, pick lint off your Club Monaco cardigan, swing your chair back and forth, twiddle your thumbs, or chew gum. You get the picture.

___

⑥   Make eye contact. Do not look at the floor, or the walls. You're talking about yourself, what your hopes and dreams are. You want to land this job. If your eye wanders off, your potential employer will lose interest and focus on what you're fixated on.

___

⑦   Remain positive when interviewing. Send the message that you will go beyond what's expected. Do not say you're thinking of assisting for a year and then turning your attention to designing a bag line. (I've heard this before!) Talk about how you complete projects thoroughly, about your time management and organizational skills. Tell your interviewer what motivates you to work; your passions; how you've worked previously on a team or independently; how you handle stress when something goes wrong.

___

⑧   No one likes to discuss salary requirements. But it's best to be straightforward and best to ask for—not demand— what you're worth and see what happens. I always ask for a bit more, knowing that I will be offered less. Make sure you're asking for a salary you feel comfortable with and not out of the realm of possibility. Fashion magazine editorial work usually pays less than other styling gigs, but you do get some great perks, such as freebies and discounts. You'll also get invaluable experience. I have never been in it for the money. I started in 1986 at around $17,000 a year doing editorial work. As an assistant this meant I cleaned fashion closets and coffee mugs along with doing mini-market call-ins. I loved every minute and I made hardly any money.

___

⑨   Don't gossip. It's just not worth it. Anyway, most of the dirt on stylists is already well known. If you've worked with someone who went off her meds and went nutty, everyone knows it already. You do not need to add fuel to the fire. Be professional and convey that you're loyal to your employers, past and present.

(10) Follow up with a thank-you note. Yep. On a real note card—not memo paper, Post-its, Hello Kitty stationery, or something that's scented or has stickers (seriously, I've received these!).

PAYING YOUR DUES

As with all jobs, the beginner stylist, assistant, or apprentice starts at the bottom. You'll have to work your butt off to earn trust and develop strong professional relationships. It will help if you really love your internship or assistant job. Love it so much that you're okay with getting paid nothing or very little in the beginning. The good news is that if you truly work hard at it, an internship can lead to another job. If the word gets out that you're really dedicated, people will want to help you. It's a great reflection on a boss when you're promotable. If you've proven yourself for little or no pay, your commitment comes across. A good boss will feel some responsibility to help you find a great placement.

Your first couple of years will be difficult, but if you hold on tight to your dream, stay focused, and handle the pressure, you'll fulfill those long-term goals.

PORTRAIT OF AN ENTRY-LEVEL POSITION

So what's a typical entry-level job like? What can you look forward to? To begin with, a lot of grunt work. You will be held responsible for taping, tacking, and sewing an actress into a dress; you'll be the one who makes sure that the double-stick tape is properly stuck to the plunging cleavage and the one who will schlep a rack of low-hanging gowns up a canyon road, alone. Even though you're called an assistant, you're more like a secretary because you'll be answering phones, picking up the dry cleaning, fetching Frappuccinos, and, in some cases, even being a part-time nanny to your boss's kid.

Because your job is in high demand, I can guarantee that there is someone all too willing waiting in the wings. Don't assume your boss would be lost without you. It's likely your boss has been through heinous situations, bosses, and drama him- or herself. Whatever you're going through is probably nothing like what he or she has lived through, so don't even try looking for sympathy.

You may be working for someone who is a stressed-out drama queen. It's likely that your family cannot understand why why why you put up with it. But it's the way of the styling world. All of today's major stylists were trained by demanding stylists. The reason they're so successful today is that they handled the drama and the insanity. They didn't quit even if they were treated like hell. Many aspiring stylists I meet don't succeed because they won't give a new job longer than two months before they're out the door. In my opinion, if you're not stretched, you're not challenged.

KEEPING YOUR COOL

So how do you get through the difficult phase of interning or assisting? Here are a few tips to keep in mind on every job you endure.

Never throw your boss under the bus. Bad-mouthing and backstabbing ultimately get you nowhere. Your verbal diarrhea will get you in even more troubled water if your boss catches wind of it, which he or she usually will.

Don't take it personally. I am the first to admit that in the early years of my career I took absolutely everything personally. I'm a creative and dramatic human being, and this got me in trouble. The screaming, throwing, and tantrums—all of your boss's insanity—usually has nothing to do with

FROM INTERN TO ASSISTANT

WHEN I WORKED AT *HARPER'S BAZAAR* as the fashion market director, I handled all the clothing coming in and out of Paris for the magazine. We hired several interns and assistants, including Charlotte Ronson and Tory Burch, who have gone on to create their own hugely successful fashion lines. After their internships were over, we helped place our girls at the big fashion houses throughout the city: Donna Karan, Chanel, Dior, Helmut Lang, Calvin Klein, Versace, and Isaac Mizrahi. They were beautifully trained, and later they got us whatever we needed for shoots! Everyone won.

you. Say the wrong thing and boom! It's all on you . . . but is it? Try as best as you can to let things roll off your back.

Be available 24/7. You must make yourself available at all hours. Stylists don't get Saturday and Sunday off. You'll get called on weekends, during vacations, and at midnight. It's just the way the business rolls nowadays.

Don't expect praise, pats on the back, or acknowledgment. Why? Because sometimes you'll work with people who are great at acknowledging your work, and sometimes you won't. Pouting is not going to solve anything. Remind yourself that you're in this for the experience.

The truth always wins. Always. It's simply not worth it to lie. You should be forthcoming, handle a crisis by immediately taking responsibility, and then move on.

Choose your battles. Before you enter into the war zone, make sure you have a great reason why you're headed into the trenches. Be mature and don't get catty. It's not professional to act nasty, and no one has time to deal with any of that craziness anyway. Styling jobs are scarce, and yes, you should feel lucky that you were the chosen one.

Take pride in your work. You're running around like a crazy person, trying to get it all done, taking the calls, running the operation. You may not be getting much credit, but you should still take great pride in your work. Make yourself the best assistant you can be. Kristen Turner, who assists stylists in Los Angeles, told me: "Stay focused. It's hard to break in to this industry, but if you're focused, you can become one of the best stylists. It's important that you are diligent and take pride in your work. Even if you're assisting, play as if it's your job or client and put your best foot forward. If you're asked to steam, do the best damn steaming anyone's ever seen. People take note, and you'll quickly be in high demand."

Listen and learn! The best way to succeed is to shut up for a few minutes and really listen. Take notes. It may sound silly, but never be without a pad and pen. Write things down, as there are so many details that'll be thrown at you.

WHEN TO CALL IT QUITS

How do you know when to leave a gig? Every stylist says assisting for at least two years is essential. It takes that long to really learn the basics. Sure, you may luck out and get big jobs sooner than that, but there's no guarantee.

Though assisting can be grueling, you shouldn't leave a job just because something goes wrong or someone hurts your feelings. Think about why you're upset: You couldn't get a gown from a designer? A bead fell off a dress and you couldn't get it fixed? Don't be a ding-dong. Keep things in perspective. Find a way to make it work.

Ask yourself a few questions. Has the boss been harping on you for a reason? Have you been behaving badly? Have you been banned from a showroom or designer? Has a client's publicist complained about the way you do business? If you're at fault, see if you can turn the situation around. But if you absolutely can't make it work, it may be time to leave. But all is not lost. Try to leave on good terms and keep in mind that even though this particular situation didn't work out, you've learned from the job. Don't burn bridges. You need every reference you can get. Ideally, before you leave you'll have figured out a plan and have another job lined up. Every job has its pitfalls. Sometimes a bad experience makes for the best learning experience—you'll figure out how to do things better the next round.

A word to the wise: If you can't tough it out, maybe this isn't the business for you. Everyone in the styling industry is very passionate and most will do whatever it takes to get and keep the job. If you don't have that drive, whether it's for styling, fashion editorial, or wardrobe, maybe this isn't the right path for you. I'm not suggesting you put up with abuse or sexual harassment. But I am suggesting you keep a stiff upper lip and positive outlook.

Annie Ladino, who has styled Becki Newton, told me: "Be professional, show your enthusiasm, and always do your best no matter how demeaning any task may be. Having a good attitude goes a long way in the end." If you learn how not to repeat the same mistakes, you too can mentor someone. Keep everything in perspective—remember it's fashion, it's fun, and it's forever changing.

Q & A WITH MONICA ROSE

Los Angeles–based stylist Monica Rose keeps herself incredibly busy dressing all the Kardashian girls (and mom Kris) as well as juggling her other clients and editorial work.

WHY DID YOU BECOME A STYLIST?

Where I'm from, people don't really get into fashion. There were no reality shows about stylists when I was young, so I wasn't even aware of what a *stylist* was. I didn't even realize I was *styling* until later. But that's what I loved doing. One day a photographer asked me if I would work with him on some test shoots, and that was it. I just knew that was what I wanted to do and it came very natural to me.

TELL ME ABOUT THE CHALLENGES OF THE JOB.

Sometimes you do a fitting and you just know you haven't nailed it yet. So you have to go out and find even better options. When Kim [Kardashian] did the Emmys this year, her dress ripped right before she went on the red carpet and we had to sew her in it! Getting the wardrobe can be very difficult sometimes, but somehow it always comes together. I'm always up for a challenge.

WHAT IS IT THAT MAKES PEOPLE THINK WHAT YOU DO IS SIMPLE, EASY, AND GLAMOROUS?

Styling is still pretty foreign to most people. People see an editorial or a celebrity on the red carpet and think, "I can do that!" They don't see weeks of preparation, cars full of garment bags, late-night fittings, tailoring, returns, et cetera.

WHAT WORDS OF ADVICE WOULD YOU HAVE FOR YOUNG PEOPLE WHO DREAM OF DOING WHAT YOU DO?

My advice is never give up. If you work hard and set your mind to it, you will make it. Focus is key. Don't worry about everybody else; it's a waste of time to worry about someone else making it before you. Your time will come if you're on the right path. I also suggest working in retail, interning, and assisting. Don't expect to one day decide to style and the next have an A-list client walk the red carpet. Also, don't go into it thinking you are going to make a ton of money right away. It's all about timing and patience.

WHAT'S YOUR BIGGEST STYLING TIP OR SECRET?

Know what works with your body. You can always enhance your body with a good tailor and Spanx, but don't try to wear something that does not flatter your body type. From skinny to curvy, every shape is beautiful, but it's knowing what to hide and what to show off that makes every outfit sexy. Look at celebrities with similar body types for inspiration.

TELL ME ABOUT THE STYLE EVOLUTION OF KIM KARDASHIAN. THE PAST TWO YEARS SHE'S MADE BEST-DRESSED LISTS, WHICH WASN'T THE CASE IN THE PAST.

Kim is amazing to work with because she loves to take fashion risks. When you have a client who loves to try new things, it makes everything just come together. She and I refined her sexy edginess to the point where, when you look at her, she looks comfortable in her clothing. It's very important for the client to feel beautiful and confident. When that happens, anything looks great on her, and you are definitely doing your job as a stylist.

DO YOU WORK WITH THE ENTIRE KARDASHIAN FAMILY?

I work with Kris, Kourtney, Kim, and Khloe. They all know what they like and what makes them feel fab and sexy. I just help them create the looks that work with their body and style.

CHAPTER THREE

On the Job!

Now it's time to get to work. Assuming this is your first day on the job, let's look at what's expected of you and how to succeed. Everything happens at a very rapid pace, so you really need to get that thinking cap on fast. Do not babble and do not take your sweet time. A lot of the first few years of your core training will be juggling all sorts of tasks and information. You'll learn about clothing, jewelers, shoes, how they're all made, and who makes the best.

As a stylist's assistant, you will likely work in an office or small home doing small, odd jobs: coffee runs, dry cleaning pickups, putting travel itineraries together, dog walking, nanny service (especially if you drive, have taken CPR classes, and like kids). Seven A.M. may be your start time, and you won't leave until the entire job is done. You need to be reachable 24/7, including on weekends, by BlackBerry, iPhone, or whatever device you use. You'll be the schlepper, picking up and returning samples and clothing for shoots and press junkets and red carpet events. It's a huge part of the job. Annabel Tollman, who styles Cynthia Nixon and Jessica Simpson, told me that when assistants or interns get the job they must "be ready to work and schlep."

WHAT TO WEAR

Sure, you're an assistant and you will spend your days running around town, packing and unpacking, and doing countless other seemingly thankless acts. But you must never forget that you're a fashion assistant—not only representing yourself but your boss too. Really, do you want to do a pickup from the Dolce store looking hungover? No, you do not.

And so I present you with the assistant essentials courtesy of New York's own wise power stylist June Ambrose. Her client roster includes Jay-Z, Missy Elliot, Mariah Carey, and Mary J. Blige. No matter what the weather or the type of job, June's always dressed to the nines. Here's her wardrobe cheat sheet:

Lanvin flats: You will never be wrong or, more important, uncomfortable in this classic shoe. Never.

Harem pants: Think of these as fashion's sweatpants. Comfortable chic always wins.

Cashmere cardigan: Layering, layering, layering. It's just another version of "Be prepared."

All black: You spend your time dressing other people. Keep it simple when it comes to yourself. It's not your job to stand out. You'd be smart to always remember this nugget.

The bag: There will never, ever be enough room in your bag. So the bigger and chic-er, the better.

MetroCard: Everyone's New York essential. When you need to pick up seven pairs of Louboutins yourself and cabs are too slow and pricey, subway is THE way to go!

Ambrose also says, "I am a recessionista! Why wouldn't I be? Of course I love Zara, Club Monaco, and Chanel, but hey, I am realistic. If like I like it, I like it, and if something is made well, and if it's of good quality, then I'll rock it. There are so many respected designers doing lower-end lines, everyone from Malandrino to Anna Sui, you can't help but become a recessionista . . . and still look fabulous!"

For another take on your work wardrobe, here's Ambrose's take on everything you need to know about East Coast stylist style:

Accessories: These are an extension of your own personal style and taste. They add the perfect punctuation to the simplest of outfits.

Bold fur or faux coat: This type of outerwear will fashionably protect you from the chill of the winter while you are hustling and bustling on the job.

Platform boots: In knee or thigh height, a platform boot is a working stylist's best friend. Perfect for navigating the concrete jungle.

Power suit: Always keep on hand a strong, structured power suit for last-minute meetings with clients.

Neutral-toned double-breasted coat: This article of clothing can bring classic sophistication to a casual look.

Cardigan: Throw one on to keep you modest when dishing out overt cleavage.

Peacoat: Invest in classic looks that can carry over to the next season, such as a good military peacoat.

Great schlepping must haves: Classic Chanel jacket / Petit Bateau striped top / 7 for All Mankind jeans / Lanvin flats / MetroCard (NY) / Purple Proenza Schouler bag / Hermès Birkin bag

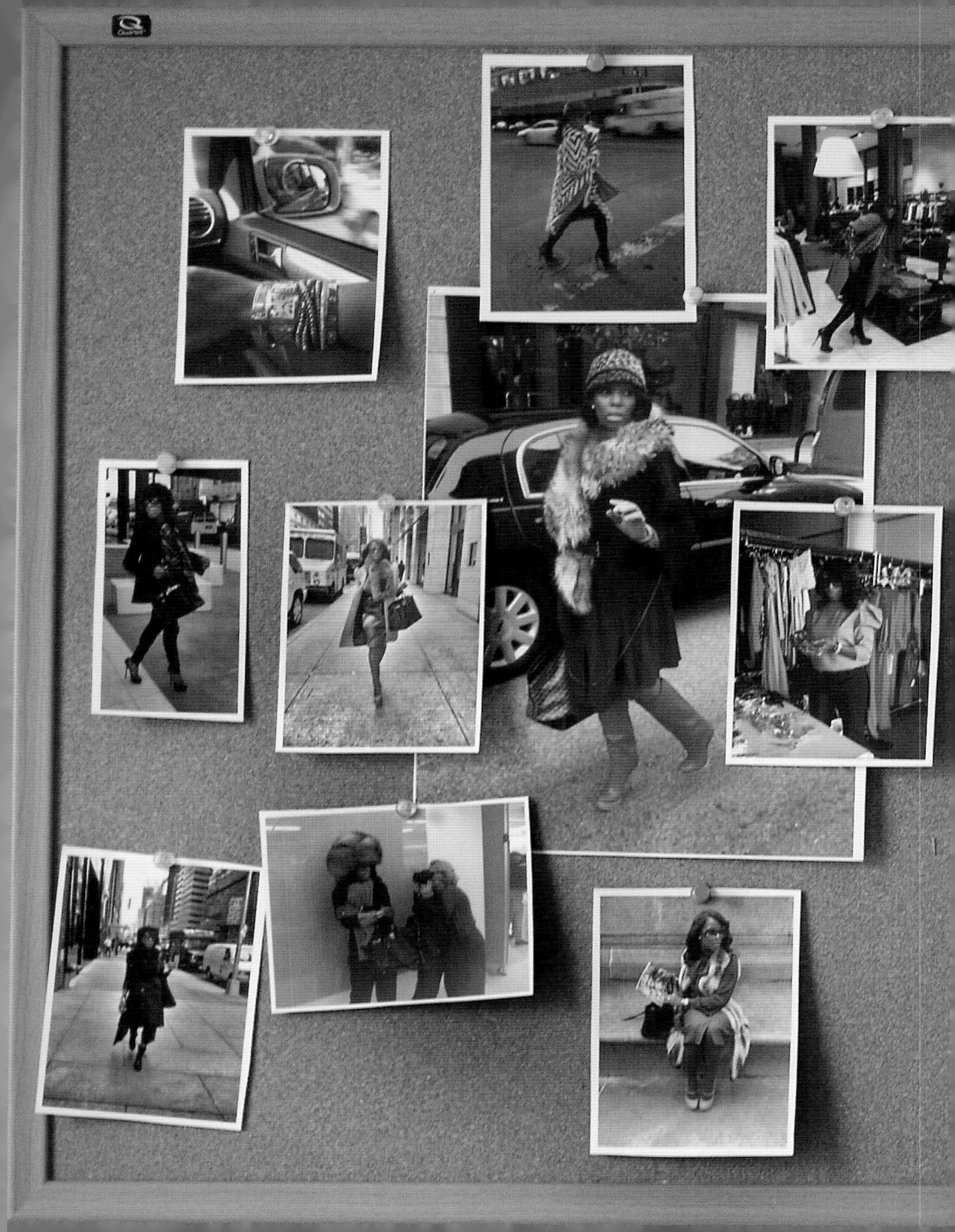

Diane Kruger works as her own stylist.

FIRST WEEK ON THE JOB

The first week on any job can be nerve racking. Here are some tips on how to get off to a good start:

Always get to your location early on your first day. Introduce yourself to everyone. Check out your surroundings. Ask questions, but don't be annoying about it: "How does the phone work for outside calls? Are there contact lists? Can I make myself a copy?" Make yourself very available: "Anything you need? What can I help with? Should I do a Starbucks or Coffee Bean run?" (*Note to self:* Ask your boss how he or she takes his or her Frappuccino, latte, or whatever ice-blended drink and size, and memorize it—you'll be ordering a ton.) Make yourself useful even if you are subjected to walking the Chihuahua, picking up dry cleaning, or fetching the kids from preschool.

Find out what the priorities are for the morning and what needs to get done immediately. 'Nuff said.

Do not speak to the celebrities! OMG, huge mistake. When my stepmother was working as creative director at *Mirabella* magazine, an assistant named Victoria was asked to man the phones for her. Victoria would pick up the calls and throw herself at the people who were calling my stepmother, saying "Oh, _____, it's me, VEEEK-TORRRRRRRRRRRRRRRIA! How are you, darling?" Oy. My stepmother's jaw would drop four inches. She was so embarrassed having to pick up the call. It was so wrong. Needless to say, Victoria was released from her position. So just put the call through. You are not going to rub elbows with Demi and Ashton at this stage in your career.

Copy and keep every cell phone number. Every means the numbers of all the assistants, VIP press, and publicists that you encounter. Why? Because your boss will call you at 11:00 P.M. looking for someone's digits. Because if you need to get in touch with Rihanna's team about which hotel she's staying in to deliver a dress, you better have the number in your cell.

Make backups of your new contacts on a computer. Cell phones commonly get left behind, or thrown at you, or dropped down a toilet. You'll be grateful you have the information backed up. Do this at the end of every week. (Also set passwords on phones so that after seven to ten tries, the phone erases personal information and starts fresh. iPhones do that after ten tries—just don't use 1-2-3-4!)

Turn that damn personal texting, AIM, and Facebook e-mailing off! There are no clever "boss buttons" to clear the screen. You shouldn't be ordering off-price Louboutins or Alaïas for yourself. Shopping online for the boss or a client is perfectly okay. But not when you're starting out, and certainly never when it feels like there's downtime. There is never downtime.

Do not dillydally. I worked for someone who actually timed her assistant to see how fast he moved clothes from a clothing rack in the fashion closet to another rack outside that closet. I've also been on shoots where an intern went AWOL for hours; she needed to go from Hollywood Boulevard to Robertson Boulevard to pick up shopping bags for a shoot—a jaunt that should've taken about thirty to forty-five minutes. After close to two hours, I called frantically because I was worried, and she said very lazily, "I'm sooo sorry. There was sooo much traffic . . ." I fell asleep before she got through the story. I didn't even let her finish.

Be honest. Do not lie. You think your boss was born yesterday? There's nothing you can say that she or he hasn't already heard or tried. The best relationships in life are built on trust, so don't blow it. Don't say you called when you

---

WATCH YOUR BACK: IT'S ALL ABOUT EVE

AHH . . . *ALL ABOUT EVE.* It's a classic movie—and the epithet muttered when a junior coworker praises you, adores you, and then stabs you in the back. Some people don't play by the rules. Those colleagues usually develop hideous reputations and fade away. But some hang on tooth and nail and, with time, all is forgiven. As long as the stylist can produce or land a huge client, people usually won't care what the person has done to get there. There's not much that can be done about this. It's a reality.

Rent *All about Eve.* It'll be the best education you'll ever get. (Plus, check out how brilliantly they dressed a very short Bette Davis!) And then recommit yourself to being an honest, trustworthy person.

didn't. And don't explain or even go into why you didn't. No one wants to hear it. Just get it done.

Be gracious. This is a job, and it will be fun and glamorous at some point. Be thankful that you have a job in a very competitive field.

THE LAY OF THE LAND

Ah, the stylist's workplace. It's a wonderland and in some cases a warehouse. You'll find shelves of shoes, or shoes lined up on the floor, as well as tables packed six deep with bags: clutches, evening minaudières, and satin and velvet purses and pouches. There'll be countless velvet-lined trays filled with bracelets, cuffs, necklaces, earrings, and rings— real and faux. Belts piled on a table. As an assistant, you will be in charge of maintaining all of it: checking items in, organizing the paperwork, knowing where everything came from so you can then send it all back.

THE RACK

One of the first things you see when you enter a stylist's workplace is "the rack." The rack is actually several racks holding dresses, gowns, coats, and jeans. You'll notice that the clothes are hung on clear, plastic, wooden, or velvet hangers—very orderly and organized. When the clothing comes in, all the bulky plastic logo hangers and wire hangers are swapped out. Really, Joan Crawford was right: she didn't want precious and expensive dresses on those terrible wire hangers.

Then all the hangers must be turned in the same direction (the hook should face away from you, not at you, so that the clothing is easier to grab). Sometimes the clothing will be lined up by color, or designer, or silhouette: tanks, camisoles, halters, shorts, miniskirts, pencil skirts, jeans, capris, wide-legged trousers, cardigans, jackets, short dresses, gowns, et cetera. You need to ask how each stylist wants his or her racks laid out.

If the racks aren't arranged in some particular way, ask your boss if this is something he or she would like you to do. If there aren't hangers, order them; you can get them from the same place you order tissue, bags, and garment bags.

Dresses on a rack getting ready for a shoot

Beautiful dresses with no wire hangers in sight

SHOES!

Shoes must be taken out of their bags and lined up in an orderly fashion. Some stylists insist on grouping them by designer, while others organize them by style: platform, peep-toe, sling backs, gladiators, flats, sandals, ballerinas, espadrilles, evening (gold, silver, and bronze together), and dyed satins. They should be lined up facing out. Never turn the shoes inward—you can't see them that way. You'll want to make sure that all shoes are tucked neatly away from rolling racks and boxes. You don't want to be billed for a platform snakeskin sandal that's been nicked by a rolling rack.

Taping the Soles

You may be borrowing shoes from a store, in which case you'll likely need to tape the bottoms so that you can return them. Taping is really easy. Find a tape that will not rip the sole to shreds. A whitish masking tape is best. I have always used Scotch's High Performance Masking tape. It's with crepe paper backing and smooth adhesive—easy for quick application—and a roll is approximately sixty yards.

Shoes lined up ready for shoots

Test it first. Always use small, sharp scissors to cut. Lay out the tape diagonally across the sole and the heel. Once you've covered the whole bottom, cut around the sole and get rid of the excess tape. Then you're done. When you remove the tape, be very careful not to damage the soles.

Also make sure when you receive the shoes that they are samples and not pulled from the store—this is usually detailed on an invoice. If they don't send one, call and check, because you'll be charged retail for the store loss.

Shoes should always face out when you are running through.

Q & A WITH SUSAN ASHBROOK

Susan Ashbrook was one of the first people to help designers put celebrities into their clothes. She is a former executive at an amazing archive and resource called Film Fashion, a premier agency matching A-list celebrities with exclusive fashion designers. Today, almost every major design house has a "celebrity division" or V.I.P. position based on this concept.

WHAT'S YOUR ADVICE TO YOUNG PEOPLE WHO ARE JUST STARTING OUT?

They should work with a great stylist first to learn the ropes. There is more to styling than pulling clothing. They need to return borrowed clothing in a timely manner, and each piece needs to be returned as it was borrowed. You'd be surprised if I told you how many times I have seen expensive clothing wadded up at the bottom of a shopping bag. I also would advise them to watch old movies, when costume designers had the time, money, and knowledge to create custom clothing for talents that accentuated their best features—Joan Crawford's great shoulders, Lana Turner's small waist.

HOW DID YOU GET YOUR START?

I started my career in fashion working for Richard Tyler, who was the "it" designer at the time. I loved walking into his office and seeing his inspiration board full of drawings, paintings, and images from magazines that would inspire him to build a collection of clothing each season. However, I am an entrepreneur, so it wasn't long before I decided other fashion designers might want to be dressing celebrities. My clients included Ralph Lauren, Escada, Hervé Léger, Isaac Mizrahi, and later Monique Lhuillier and Alber Elbaz, among others.

WHAT WAS YOUR MISSION?

My goal was to help my clients work with actors who were established or one film away from stardom. Escada trusted my opinion enough to custom design Jennifer Lopez's wedding gown for her first marriage. The company is based in Germany and was not aware of her career yet. By the time she got married, she had four films out that year.

TELL ME ABOUT YOUR FIRST RED CARPET MOMENT.

There are many but one of my favorite moments was when Kim Basinger wore Escada to the Academy Awards. Kim had seen a photograph of an Escada gown in *Vogue* and loved it. Brian Rennie sketched some changes to the design and color to customize the gown for Kim, but with only two weeks before the Oscars, he flew over a couture seamstress to cut the muslin, make a pattern, and sew and tailor the gown to Kim's request. The seamstress was still sewing the gown as Kim walked to the limo to leave.

WHO, IN YOUR OPINION, IS MOVING FASHION FORWARD ON THE RED CARPET?

I think there are a handful of celebrities who are risk takers and have their own personal styles, like Madonna, Tilda Swinton, Kirsten Dunst, and Gwen Stefani.

WHAT WOULD YOU LIKE TO SEE MORE OF?

More dressing "high-low," which, I believe, is how more and more women are dressing, like Sharon Stone's Gap T-shirt with a fabulous pin and couture long skirt.

ACCESSORIES

Trays and trays of accessories are your responsibility to call in, unpack, pack back up, and finish.

You will receive bags and bags of accessories on a daily basis. It all needs to be checked in and counted to make sure that each of the items listed on the sheet is there. You will get charged for merchandise that's not returned. But sometimes errors occur on invoices. For example, if an accessories list notes three Louis Vuitton foxtail-fur key chains in green, pink, and blue, but you received only two, you need to call right away so that you're protected.

Because there's so much out there that looks the same, it's essential that you know what's what and who made it. Devise a check-in system that works for you. For instance, take photos of what comes in, or write up a list and then make a copy. Attach the invoice and the count of merchandise. Create folders and organize them by designer.

Trays and trays of fine and costume jewelry are called in for shoots. Jewelry should always be laid out on black velvet trays, so you can check them in and know what you have to work with.

Leighton Meester and Blake Lively on the streets of NYC, filming the TV show *Gossip Girl*, July 9, 2009

The Wardrobe/Closet on *Gossip Girl,* 2009, Long Island City, NY

RETURNING ITEMS

When the job is over, it's up to you to pack up everything neatly and return all items to the vendor, designer, or showroom. So staying organized and consistently using a system that works well for you will really pay off at the end of the day—when you don't need your headache to get even bigger because of clutter.

THE BOARD

After you've been on the job for a while you may be given the plum assignment to make a "board." I use to love and hate making boards. In the old days, we didn't have Style.com or any service to keep track of what we wanted to call in for a photo shoot. Before the Internet, we had to make Polaroids from slides. It was enormously labor intensive, but ultimately you really knew your look backward and forward because it took so damn long and you spent so much time with the visuals.

Fashion stylist Nicole Chavez, who works with Rachel Bilson and Kristen Bell, has a simple method for making boards: "First I'll think about the look I want. And then as I'm going through the collections, I'll put looks that inspire me in my little lookbook.* My assistants will print [out looks from style Web sites usually from Style.com], cut them up, and, on the back, write the collection and the look number. Then I look at everything they've put together in the lookbook. I kind of edit this way. The designers e-mail me about what is or isn't available—usually about a third of the looks aren't available. We remove the unavailable looks, substitute in the available looks, move them around. Then I'll know exactly what's coming in for my fitting. I'm not surprised." Want to hear more from Chavez? Check out her interview on page 56.

*A *lookbook* that's made by a stylist is a notebook or binder in which stylists place all of their inspirational loose magazine sheets. They can then go back and look at these pictures for reference or outfit ideas, or feelings and thoughts for the red carpet or a fashion shoot. A lookbook from a designer highlights every outfit that comes down the runway and is numbered. Plus, there are several pictures of accessories in the back of the book to get a full-picture idea of what the season is about.

SETTING UP A BOARD

Here are six basic steps to assembling a board on your own:

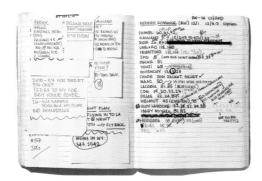

I used lined notebooks to keep track of what was coming in for shoots, and I still do. I update with Post-its. Don't rely on a computer because documents can get lost!

① Go to Style.com to search for fashion shows. These are arranged by season, with the most recent highlighted first. The seasons are Fall-Winter, Spring-Summer, Haute Couture (Spring and Fall), Pre-Fall, Pre-Spring, and Resort. The seasons are broken down into Ready to Wear (dresses, coats, pants, gowns, etc.), Couture, Resort, Pre-Fall, Menswear, Designer Directory, and Power Search. Choose a section and have fun looking.

② Choose a designer. On the same Web site, you can read a review of any collection. Or, to see all the pictures from a collection, select the Complete Collection tab. Click on the first "look." Every outfit that comes down a runway has an assigned number. Pick your looks, note the numbers, then go on to other designers.

③ Print your looks. Don't forget outfits, accessories, bags, shoes, and details. Then cut the pictures out, making sure that the look number is visible—otherwise it will be a bitch trying to figure out the look number later on. Write the designer on the bottom, far right, or the back of the printout and tack that on the board.

④ Organize the board by designer. Tack on your looks using the same color tacks (I prefer clear). Make sure that the looks are grouped by designer and are in sequential order.

⑤ Add personal pictures. These might include samples that were photographed at an appointment, for instance a dress that hasn't been shown on the runway or a collection of scarves. Images of jewelry from showrooms go on this board or on a separate jewelry and accessories board.

⑥ Call it in! Do this once you get all the designers and accessories up on the board. And of course, log it all in. I have kept all of my old books.

THE MARKET

Where does all this delicious stuff come from? It comes from a wonderful place called the *market,* a term for the designers, ateliers, and showrooms from which you can get all of the samples, clothing, shoes, and accessories. The market is a huge territory.

To begin, set up a market appointment. Then go to the showroom and "pull" looks, which means that, after looking at dozens of dresses, gowns, and jewelry, you will literally pull them off the rack and into your clutches. You will do a swift edit—not take the entire showroom with you—fill out paperwork, and leave with a few excellent looks.

When creating your own look, I strongly advise doing the pulling yourself. Only you will have a clear idea of exactly what you need. Sending someone else to check it out or do the "shopping" is risky, because she or he won't know the background of your story or the right colors, cuts, or idea.

Try to beg or borrow from showrooms, because it's difficult to get budgets for clothing unless a studio or magazine is fronting the bill. Typically there is an unwritten agreement that designers are lending you the clothes so that they will get "free publicity," meaning their pieces will get photographed and the designer will be credited in print. Or a celebrity will be trained to say who she or he is wearing when they walk on a carpet. Or you alert a designer showroom that a certain celebrity wore the dress; the showroom will then send out a press release to the media that a particular dress was worn at such and such event, including information on the designer.

You will pull many things that never see the light of day on the carpet or at the shoot. And as disappointing as it is, the designers and the showrooms are used to that. For awards shows or personal appearances, there's a lot of running around town and making calls to reserve gowns as soon as possible so as not to miss out on the best looks. You'll find there is usually one dress that everyone wants. Celebrities, magazines, department stores, and buyers all have to compete with one another to see who can get that happening dress first.

Just as you've borrowed and begged for looks, you absolutely must return those samples. You can completely ruin your reputation if you steal, neglect to return, roll into balls and shove in a paper bag, or give a friend the clothing to wear, which ends up being seen at a party or on Facebook. You could get yourself in a lot of trouble. Be sure to treat the clothing with respect. This is a business.

STUDIO SERVICES

Say you have a particular look in mind but can't beg, borrow, or get a loaner. This is when you go to studio services. Most of the big stores offer this service—Barneys, Saks, Neiman Marcus, Bloomingdales, and Bergdorf Goodman, to name a few.

Make an appointment to meet with a service representative. They take appointments with anyone, but you must observe their rules and provide a credit card for deposits. As part of the agreement, you will be required to purchase some of the items you borrow. When you get to studio services, you'll check out purchases with the staff member. They'll ask for your credit card, business card, and possibly a letter of responsibility.

Stylist George Kotsiopoulos, who has worked with Britney Spears and the actress Freida Pinto, told me that when he's out to purchase clothing for special assignments, he first goes to the studio services department to take the clothes out on approval. The deal is that he must then buy between 15 and 20 percent of what he pulls. Advantage: You get what you want, if it's there, and you get to keep it for a week. Disadvantage: "You have to look at retail price tags when you pull! I hate being limited by what things cost. I always want to shoot the most current and most beautiful things, and these usually come at a price," said Kotsiopoulos.

APPROVED/NOT APPROVED

MUCH LIKE APPLYING FOR A CREDIT CARD and either getting that credit line or not, there is an unwritten list of celebrities who are approved to wear certain designer clothing and ones who you are not allowed to pull for. A former press rep told me, "It was never put in writing but we were definitely not crazy about a handful of pop stars, reality television stars, and a few celebutantes. Often we were the ones to decide—and the home office trusted us. We were going by gut a lot of times." Another problem arises when you want a Sarah Jessica or Angelina to wear a designer's piece but they've seen it on every Tom, Dick, and Harriet. They're not going to want to wear it. This is when studio services at the big stores come in handy. Your celebrity will get to see the big labels and you won't run into trouble.

Q&A WITH LAURA MANNIX

I had the great fortune to speak with Laura Mannix who is the director of Studio Services at Barneys New York. Here we discussed how to call in looks and navigate Studio Services.

WHAT EXACTLY IS STUDIO SERVICES?

Studio services is a unique niche of retail that is devoted to costume designers, stylists, and editors. Costume designers use Studio Services to create comprehensive character-driven wardrobes for movies and television. Stylists use it to outfit casts and models for advertising projects and for celebrity styling—be it for press junkets, special appearances, or photo shoots.

HOW EXACTLY DOES STUDIO SERVICES WORK?

It is appointment based and we usually pre-shop or shop with the stylist to create total looks. Many clients have been working with studio services since its inception at Barneys in 1995. We are so familiar with their style and vision that we often edit the store before they come in or call them when we have some complete looks for them to see. Studio Services is fast-paced and energizing. It's a clubhouse of the most creative and inspiring people in the industry—people who set trends through television, film, and magazines.

WILL YOU GIVE US SOME TIPS ON WORKING SUCCESSFULLY WITH STUDIO SERVICES?

- Make an appointment!
- Treat the merchandise with respect.
- Discuss any special needs or adjustments PRIOR to leaving with your looks.
- Be polite. Remember, you are one of many clients having an "emergency" otherwise known as styling.
- Bring cupcakes. Sweets are always appreciated, and may lead to special treatment.

SECURING THE LOOKS

You've decided what you want for the shoot, event, or junket based on all the looks you pulled. Now you'll need to properly secure the outfit. Send a request to the press office of the designer for the look. You must provide the date of the event, how long the look will be out, and when you're going to return it.

One very important note: Just because you've secured a look for a celebrity doesn't mean that another stylist hasn't secured that same look for another celebrity client.

After you put in the request, you'll get a call or an e-mail confirming availability and when the looks will be ready for pickup. If you need a look from another city or country, the process gets more complicated; items will need to be shipped via FedEx or Worldnet, or via carnet if coming from overseas, so factor in the extra time.

When you get confirmation of what looks are available, be sure to log what's coming in and what's not on the board; using sticky notes in a nice, organized way is a great way to do this. Immediately tell your boss what's not going to be possible and why. You may have to pick up the looks yourself from a hotel, boutique, or an editor at a shoot. Keep in mind that editors have a hard time letting go of samples as well as returning them. They often move clothing from shoot to shoot without approval from the designer. Samples are shared globally, so when it's due for return, someone else is likely waiting for it. You are not allowed to move clothing you have reserved for one celebrity to another celebrity, because the designer may not have approved the other celeb.

When the clothing comes in, you'll likely receive a listing from the showroom it came from. Read it, log it in, and check to see that all items are accounted for. Also check to see if there are snags, rips, or stains. If you find anything amiss, call the showroom or designer immediately and report the damage. They will bill you the full retail price of the dress if you don't report the damage.

When you return the clothing, do so in a timely manner. If your boss wants to hold on to the clothes longer, you must have it approved by the showroom. If not, you'll hear from a shrieking publicist, showroom staffer, or designer, because someone else is likely waiting for it. It's imperative to maintain healthy and happy relationships with the market and designers. The best way to guarantee positive relations is to handle items in a timely and tidy manner.

RECEIVING AND RETURNING THE LOOKS

Here are a few tips on receiving and returning items:

① Maintain a log. Create a system to track what you received and what you're returning. Highlight each item and confirm that it has arrived or is being returned, so that you have a record. You can also take a digital picture of arrivals and returns for clear-as-crystal backup.

② Keep things neat. Follow a system for changing hangers, hanging clothing, and laying clothes out. Be efficient and thorough. Bosses and stylists go nuts when assistants take forever to hang things.

WHO WORE IT BETTER?

IT HAPPENS: two celebs show up wearing the same dress. This is the trademarked section of *Us Weekly* that I gratefully inherited as part of my job. I love sorting through pictures and events for celebrities dressed in identical dresses.

Even when walking down the street I can't help but look at regular people with this *Us Weekly* feature in mind. Inevitably I'll come across someone in the same DVF polka-dot top as Nicky Hilton *and* Lauren Conrad.

How do you prevent another person from wearing your client's look? There's absolutely nothing you can do once a dress from the runway has been commercialized for sale. At that point, everyone has access to buy it, throw it on his or her back, and make appearances.

So Amanda Bynes may have borrowed a pink bandage Hervé Léger dress from the showroom, but since it's available at the retailer Intermix, Denise Richards's assistant or personal shopper may buy that same dress. When Denise pops up on my screen wearing it, it's my job to remember who wore it before. Usually neither girl is aware that they *both* had the same dress on . . . until we or some other magazine exposes it.

There also can be problems when a European house puts Lindsay Lohan in a denim dress overseas and

③ For paper bag returns: Fold dresses and clothing neatly. I shouldn't have to say this, but I will: Do not roll up a couture gown into a wad. Make sure that if you use stickers to address the bag for a messenger, you write the return neatly and with a ballpoint pen. Inky pens may run onto clothing and destroy something.

④ For garment bag returns: Keep clothing neatly hung in the garment bag and follow the same labeling directions as for paper bag returns.

⑤ For carnet returns: Be sure to line everything with tissue before shipping.

If, God forbid, you lose something, don't panic. If you've double-checked your records and still can't find the item, approach your boss, explain the steps you've taken to find it, and see what happens. Sometimes a stylist is charged, and sometimes not. Be prepared. George Kotsiopoulos told me: "If it's beyond your control when something gets lost or damaged or doesn't arrive on time for the shoot, just wing it."

After you pull the looks from the showrooms, the next step is the fitting. When you're working with real-size clients (meaning: not models), you may need to borrow or buy from a store. Runway samples are cut for the model. If you want it for your client, you must make sure that you can fit him or her into a subzero-size garment.

A tailor can make alterations, letting garments in or out, but if you have a size 12 celebrity who may actually be closer to a 14, and you ordered only looks 16 and 83 from the Giorgio Armani Privé haute couture collection, you're going to have a huge problem, because they will not fit. You do not want to risk embarrassing your celebrity at her fitting, or make her the laughingstock of the Internet and the weeklies in an ill-fitting gown—no matter how much your star begs for that particular look.

Even if you have a great tailor, it's still important for stylists to know about fit and drape. Deborah Waknin says that knowing about drape, cut, and fit are essential to a stylist's success. She explains: "It is absolutely imperative. Not only do you need a great seamstress, but a stylist needs to understand how the dress is going to fall and whether it's a bias cut, a satin-back drape, or a silk jersey. You have to understand the drape of a dress in order to get it to fit properly. You must educate yourself. Take a draping class and a sewing class. It's what gives you a good eye."

One way that stylists avoid a fitting mishap is by hiring assistants who are the size and shape of their clients and using them as the "fit" model. Robert Verdi has two assistants who are the shape and height of two of his clients: Eva

meanwhile, an American press office has a duplicate collection and puts Eva Longoria in that same dress for a Rome appearance on the same night. Or when Shakira and Pink show up on the red carpet of the MTV Video Music Awards in the same Balmain dress two minutes apart. Sometimes it just happens.

Most of the time it's an honest mistake. But other times, certain celebs and stylists have been known to repeat someone else's look to get press. Such individuals know what's been previously worn, since many showrooms tag a dress with that sort of information. But they'll still pull the look and put their client in it. Oy.

There have been a few rare occasions when a dress that was meant for one celebrity ended up on another, with happy consequences. For instance, when Nicole Richie ended up at her court appearance in the Moschino dress originally meant for Jessica Biel, everything worked out. She showed up in court looking like Audrey Hepburn, and the photo was seen everywhere, bringing lots of attention to Moschino.

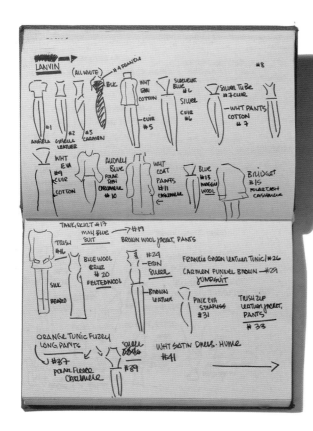

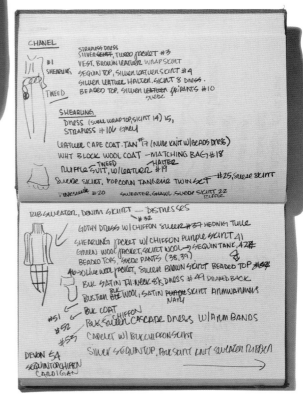

My vintage sketch books from fashion shows helped me remember what I saw and what I liked.

WHAT IS A CARNET?

I WON'T SUGARCOAT IT. A carnet is, quite frankly, a pain in the ass. But a very necessary one. Each article of clothing practically gets its own passport. A carnet (car-nay) is an international customs document that allows you to carry or send merchandise for up to one year into another country without paying duties, or submitting the normal customs documents. Which is why a carnet can be a better option than sending via other shipping services. The carnet is valid in approximately fifty countries throughout Europe, North America, Asia, and Africa. Costs will generally be between $200 and $400.

When I was an editor at *Harper's Bazaar,* I thought I was going to lose my job waiting for clothing coming via carnet for a shoot. This carnet was held up in U.S. Customs and never released because of a pair of sunglasses! (Apparently, when I innocently listed UVA and UVB on the carnet for these high-end sunglasses, it caused the customs officers to get the Food and Drug Administration involved.)

Longoria and Kathy Griffin. Fit models are helpful when you need to pre-fit dresses before your client arrives, to see how things will sit, how much tacking and tailoring you're actually going to need, and if it's simply not going to work. Many stylists hire girls from modeling agencies with the same measurements as their clients to do the first fittings.

Stylist Penny Lovell's process of making memorable looks on the red carpet requires working closely with her clients. "After lots of researching collections, I call in looks I like—that are available for the client—choose my preferences, and then do a collaborative fitting with my client." Nicole Chavez, who works with Kristen Bell, Rachel Bilson, and Scarlett Johansson says, "We decide on looks and pin and tailor. Sometimes we do second fittings to check tailoring, depending on how much needed to be done. I would say for a whole tour or press junket, we tailor around 85 percent of everything—it really is the secret to red carpet dressing. We generally find the perfect accessories after the fitting when we know exactly what we're looking for. For press tours we do a couple of different fittings. We always take pictures of every potential outfit to see how they will look on camera and to use for researching accessories."

WHEN A LOOK DOESN'T FIT

As gorgeous as celebrities are, most can't fit into runway samples. Most runway samples are cut for fourteen-year-old supermodels. So what happens when Versace arrives and it doesn't work? Stylist Jonny Lichtenstein, who works with Sigourney Weaver, told me how to arm yourself for fit issues: "The best thing to do is prepare in advance. Make sure you have at least one fitting prior to the event; never assume the alterations are going to be perfect. Have a seamstress on hand to tweak anything right before the event. If you have no time, have a backup dress that you know will

fit. Don't be afraid to ask the publicist who works directly with the celebrity a million questions. Get the most recent measurements—you can get these from the film's costume department—ask the publicist what colors to avoid, which ones the celebrity loves, which designers she or he wears, and bring enough options."

You may also find yourself styling an older, more mature celebrity. Lichtenstein is an expert in this arena. He told me: "The challenge with dressing more mature women is

Q & A WITH NICOLE CHAVEZ

California native Nicole Chavez started in film but eventually got a big break working on The OC. *She became fast friends with star Rachel Bilson, whom she soon began styling. She also works with Kristen Bell and Scarlett Johansson.*

HOW LONG DO FITTINGS USUALLY TAKE?

It depends on the client. But on average, fifteen looks will probably take an hour and a half to two hours. I have the tailor there. And I take digital photos so I can see what's working and what's not. And then I just keep everything pinned. Then I'll download the pictures, look at everything, and edit that way too. Then I send [the garment] to the tailor to be altered. Everything gets altered. I don't think I've ever sent anyone down the red carpet without it being pinned.

HOW MANY PEOPLE ARE ON YOUR TEAM?

I have an assistant and an intern. And I sometimes have a third assistant running around if it gets really busy.

DO YOU COLLABORATE WITH HAIR AND MAKEUP TO FIGURE OUT THE OVERALL LOOK?

Absolutely. It's a team effort when you deal with me. First, I work with the publicist to get a very detailed list of exactly where the client is going to be, what she is doing. I want to know whether she'll be standing or sitting and in what kind of chair. Because it makes a huge difference. I'm not going put someone in a miniskirt who's going to be sitting on a chair. That's when I'll slot in the looks for the events. Then I e-mail hair and makeup to give them details on the looks for the different events; then they at least know and are on board.

AND USUALLY THE SAME GLAM SQUAD WORKS TOGETHER?

Yes. Everyone has their same people. And we all work together. And if I am in town, I get my girls ready myself. It's totally rare that I'm not there. Like I have to have either a 101 fever or something's happened with my family or my husband. Otherwise, I'm there.

WHAT IS THE DIFFERENCE BETWEEN STYLING FOR TV AND STYLING FOR THE RED CARPET OR FOR PERSONAL STYLE?

For TV, it's a team effort. There's a costume designer, shoppers, and people who put [the look] together. There are a lot more moving parts. And the costume designer isn't the only person designing the outfits. The studio, the executive producer, and the actress or actor all have their own opinions. You're also dealing with stunts and continuity. If you have stunts, that means you've got to have four shirts. Do you have four of those shirts available? Probably not. There are a lot more things to think about when you're doing TV.

WHAT HAPPENS TO THE CLOTHES AFTER YOU'VE DONE THE WHOLE TOUR, ESPECIALLY ALTERED GARMENTS?

They go back to the designer. Or they get gifted to the girls. It depends on where they are in the collection. Usually once a garment's been worn, though, it's pretty much dead to the red carpet. It may be used for editorial, because then it doesn't matter if it's been altered. So obviously I check before altering anything. I always have the designer sign off on it beforehand.

WHAT ARE COMMON MISCONCEPTIONS OF THE JOB?

That it's easy. [The truth is that] it's fast paced, and you have to be very organized. There's no room for mistakes. You can't be lazy. You're up early, you're working on the weekends, you're always on call, you're always on your BlackBerry. People are always going to events, so there's never any downtime. You have to love it. If you do, then this is the greatest job in the world.

HOW DID YOU BUILD YOUR CLIENT BASE?

For the most part, it was built on word of mouth and just being out there. People would come to me liking [what I did for] other people with whom I've worked. It's really important for me to be passionate about the people I work with. I am so much a part of their lives, and they are so much a part of mine, that it's important that we want to work together and that we work together well.

WHO IS YOUR IDEAL ASSISTANT? WHAT WOULD YOU LOOK FOR IN SOMEONE WHO CAME TO YOU WITH VERY LITTLE EXPERIENCE?

[I'd look for someone like my intern.] She's got the ability to think ahead, think before I have to ask. She thinks like I think. She problem solves. She takes the initiative. For example, a client will e-mail her and me: "I saw these pants in *Elle* magazine. I really love them. Could you track them down?" And then I will say to my intern, "Can I leave this to you?" And she's on it. She's e-mailing my client: "This is what I found." She doesn't have to call or ask me. She gets it done. She's amazing. This weekend I had her dress somebody for the first time when I wasn't there. It's so rare that I'm not there, but it was my anniversary. She did a great job. You've got to let them spread their wings a little bit and do their thing.

It's taking the initiative before someone has to ask you, and knowing when to share your opinion. Because all of what we do is in our heart and in our head, so everyone has a different opinion. As a stylist, if I'm talking to a client about what I think about the look, I don't need my assistant's opinion. But I ask her, "Well, what do you think?" It's being careful with your words and knowing when it's right to speak and when it's not. I learned that when I worked on set. You learn how to talk with clients and know what's the right thing to say, like how to work your way through uncomfortable situations if someone doesn't want to wear something and you don't have the power to change it. You have to know how to do that.

It also helps to have taken a psychology class, because the mind games in this business are crazy! The personalities that you're dealing with are off the charts. So you really have to be able to roll with stuff and not take things so personally, and also just be positive. Being a team player goes a long way in this business.

WHAT INFLUENCES YOU? WHAT DO YOU LOVE TO LOOK AT, BEYOND COLLECTIONS?

Movies. I pick so much from movies, old movies and all movies in general. And art. I love Impressionist art. Fanciful, expressive, dreamlike art is what I love. And I love abstract art.

DO YOU FEEL YOU'RE PART STYLIST AND PART PERSONAL SHOPPER?

No. I don't do personal shopping. If a girl likes something, that's usually a job for my intern. She's the queen of finding anything. So I just hand it over to her because again, I'm too busy.

WHAT IS YOUR BEST-KEPT STYLING SECRET?

Tailoring. I can tell when people get their clothes from the showroom. I can tell when things don't fit properly. I don't only fit a garment to the body, I also make adjustments for their body type. If it needs to be shorter or longer, if the neckline needs to be sweetheart or square, I make all those adjustments. Sometimes I'm redesigning a little bit to make it work. We're all different shapes and sizes, and some things just look different on different people. I think tailoring is essential.

WHAT DO YOU LOVE MOST ABOUT WHAT YOU DO?

I love that it's different every day. I just love the whole process. I think it's really incredible to be able to work with art every day and create it and be a part of it. It's an amazing experience.

to make sure you really listen to them and work with their existing style rather than trying to change it completely. There is a reason they have lasted so long in the industry, and their style, good or bad, is a part of their image. So you must take this into account when choosing clothing. You can elevate or modify style, but you must listen to these women and make sure they stay true to themselves."

For the best designer for more generous figures, or for the more mature woman, Lichtenstein said: "When in doubt, Donna Karan works every time! She understands a woman's body and is the master of masking problem areas with ruching and draping. Stretch jersey is a stylist's best friend."

ACCESSORIZING

One thing I love love love about fashion is that you can make a lovely dress into an extraordinary iconic look with the help of accessories. It's about playing with jewelry and knowing what works. Lee Harris told me that when he works with Drew Barrymore, he thinks "the proper jewelry can really send an outfit over the top in a successful way. Drew has amazing taste in jewelry, so I am always trying to find new and interesting pieces for her. She wore a white jersey Donna Karan draped gown to her *Music and Lyrics* premiere in NYC, and I think the pearl Steven Dweck necklace really made the whole outfit sing. The same goes for the wristful of gold Ofira bracelets she wore to the same premiere in L.A. The bracelets were actually Drew's concept; it was my job to source out such a large number of bracelets from one designer."

JEWELRY

Most jewelry worn on the red carpet is borrowed and rarely owned, but it has the power to set trends. For instance, when stylist Jen Rade adorned Angelina Jolie with beautiful dangling emerald earrings at the Academy Awards in 2009, the Lorraine Schwartz $2.5 million emerald drops not only set off a trend, they made for an iconic red carpet moment.

Lorraine Schwartz emerald earrings that became iconic

STYLING TIPS FOR MEN

IF YOUR MALE CLIENT is going to the trouble of going on the red carpet, it's only appropriate that you outfit him in something formal and ensure that he combs his hair, shaves, tightens up the tie, and cleans those teeth. Ditch the cummerbunds, white ties with white shirts, and the unbuttoned look. Unless he's the new Jon Hamm, skip the double-breasted suits—or he'll look boxier and bigger.

Michael Nash, who's styled Ryan Gosling and Zac Efron, shares his basics for dressing a man for the red carpet:

- *Have a backup suit.* This is the classic no-brainer if customs or FedEx or the dry cleaner makes a mistake.

PREPPING FOR THE RED CARPET

Once you've had your fittings, it's time to start thinking about the day of the big event. The best advice I can give is to prepare for the unexpected. Anything can happen, and you'll need to be armed and ready to troubleshoot any situation. Start to think about timing, how you'll work with the glam squad, and in what order your client will get hair, makeup, and wardrobe done. You'll need a prop kit (see next section) for last-minute touch-ups, and a mini sewing kit.

Make sure you do a run-through before the big event. Make doubly sure that the dress isn't transparent when your girl walks in front of a window or a lot of light. We all remember when Nicole Richie, Natalie Portman, and Anne Hathaway revealed more than they meant to in very sheer dresses. And who can forget Mariah Carey flashing everything from head to toe? A camera's flashes make many fabrics look sheer, so be certain that everything is lined and opaque. It's the stylist's responsibility to make sure everything is flawless—you'll be the one to take the heat if your celebrity looks nearly naked on the carpet. Practice with a flashlight and shine the light on the upper and lower areas of the body to make sure nothing is highlighted or transparent.

You'll also need to make sure that the celebrity has the right undergarments. If a little belly bulges out, the gossip mill will start up about pregnancy or weight gain. You can find thousands of body slimmers and belly busters on the market. Make use of them—and then make sure to run through some moves so that your client does not reveal unsightly Spanx by accident (see Sucking It In: Stylists' Magical Secrets, page 130). Taraji P. Henson had the misfortune of unintentionally raising her Cavalli gown a little too high while being interviewed by E! at the Oscars, and she revealed her underpinnings to the world. As lovely as she is, it was a bit of an embarrassment.

Remember, the red carpet is a fantastic opportunity to show off design details on the dress. If the dress has an amazing back or a low dip or side ruching, make sure that the celebrity is aware of it. They're walking billboards for designers. When they stand like a paper doll, they're not doing the dress any favors. Work it out before going on the red carpet. Practice poses with your client—one foot in front of the other, hands on hips, turn in profile—to figure out how she should stand to give the dress a great look and herself a great profile.

PROP KITS
Phillip Bloch and Paul Cavaco stylist kits

A prop kit is an assemblage of products that make a gown fit like a dream. A great prop kit will include tape for the breasts, clamps, fishing wire, stain remover, cutlets (silicone breasts that give a boost when placed inside the dress), nude pasties, shoe horn, sewing essentials, seam ripper, Static Guard, Sharpies, first-aid products, and thongs, G-strings, panties, and bras in a bevy of sizes. Will you need all of these things for a shoot or red carpet look? Not necessarily. But wouldn't you rather be prepared?

Celebrity stylist Phillip Bloch travels with a rolling bag filled with tools that can turn a so-so gown into an Oscar winner. Paul Cavaco, creative director at *Allure* magazine and my former boss and mentor, keeps a mini trunk full of tools that he restocks after each shoot. Their works are legendary, and they know everything about drape, fit, tailoring, giving direction, and how to speak to a celebrity to soothe and convince her to get into a skimpy bathing suit or a sheer-to-waist gown. I learned from them all the tools necessary to make a great look and great photo.

Manhattan Wardrobe Supply (www.wardrobesupplies .com) sells everything from hemming tape, beauty problem

---

- *Get a tailor.* The shoulders, sleeves, and length of the pants need to be handled by a professional. Do not let your client leave the house without a proper fitting or two (see Tailor Made, page 139).
- *Mirdle?* For the guy who would never get caught dead in Spanx in this or any future lifetime, you have options. A shirt with stretch in the fabric will skim off ten pounds and a spare tire. Get a tailor to slim down the shirt by darting it in the back and down the sleeves. Getting rid of that extra fabric will create less bulk under the suit and will look sharp when your client takes off his jacket.
- *Make sure the shoes fit.* Break in the shoes first, to prevent carpet slips and blisters—this will also prevent the ouch and the grouch!

solvers, and clothing to tagging guns, racks, and storage. There's even a spray you can use to get rid of wrinkles if you find yourself without an iron. If you can't make heads or tails of putting together a comprehensive kit, the company sells a premade fitting kit that includes all the essentials packed into a clear vinyl tote. And if you also need a fully inclusive kit with those very important silicone pads, pick up the Braza Diva Ultimate World Traveler kit and Manhattan Wardrobe Supply's Styling Kit.

The Braza kit includes:
- Cosmetic bag with zipper
- One pair Perki Silicone Pads
- Three Tack-Itz
- Sticky Fingers
- Two pairs Strap Keepers
- Two pairs Petal Tops
- Two pairs Reveal Adhesive Bra
- Two pairs Braza Bra

- Three pairs On the Run Disposable G-Strings
- Three Quickies Soap Wash
- Two-Hook Clear Bra Extender
- One Pair Clear Bra Straps
- The Low Down
- Two pairs Clothing Shields
- Try-On Bonnet
- One Seamless Tube Top
- One roll Flash Tape

The basic styling kit has:
- Black three-pocket apron
- One box ½-inch TopStick
- Mini lint roller
- Head scarf
- Bite Lite
- Pre-threaded needles
- Thread clipper
- Black safety pins

How does Paul Cavaco, *Allure*'s Creative Director, make a shoot work? His kit.

PHILLIP BLOCH'S KIT

I had Phillip Bloch tell me about the most important elements of his styling kit:

BELT HOLE PUNCHER:

Wow, does a belt hole puncher come in handy. As you know, a lot of R&B groups think they have a 36 waist when they really are a 32. They want everything so big. If you bring a belt with a 36 waist, it's not going to hold their pants up. I remember working with Boyz II Men on a video. I handed one of them a belt in a size 34. He really needed a 32 but told me he was a 36. He actually snapped his fingers and said, "Belt. Belt." I said, "Oh, I'm sorry." I took the belt, ripped the size tag off of it, put another hole in, and gave him back the belt and said here's your 36. But really it was a 34 with the extra hole. Then everyone was happy. Ignorant, but happy. There will be no snapping of fingers at me! Needless to say, I couldn't listen to Boyz II Men after that.

CUTLETS

Oh girl, the cutlets are the most-used item in my kit. Even though I work with full-figured curvy girls who have their own breasts, they want to push everything up to look sexier and more filled out. Cutlets are especially helpful for those who don't have much to start with. It just gives that extra little oomph. A lot of times I just have them sewn into the dress. In those cases we use foam cutlets rather than silicone.

STAPLER AND STRAIGHT PINS:

For a too-long pant hem, if I can get away with it I will use a stapler. Just two little staples on the side of each leg works wonders. If you staple vertically in a seam, no one will ever see

the evidence. Straight pins are good for a long hem of a dress if you need to mark it for the tailor. They're especially helpful when hemming a long gown and you have to pin all the way around.

BODY SHAPERS:

Body shapers are very important. Maidenform has great ones called Flexees that we use all the time. The technology is amazing. L'eggs even has some for seven bucks. I use body shapers whether the girls are skinny or fat. They feel more secure with the smoothing effects.

Mariah Carey and Phillip Bloch

STRING:

Another prized possession is a black string I wear around my neck with a collapsible silver scissor on it. I put all different sizes of safety pins on the string at the beginning of a shoot, as well as binder clips in several different sizes, and I wear that around my neck. Double-stick tape is always useful, but I prefer a safety pin.

STEAMER AND LINT ROLLER:

A handheld steamer is a necessity. And no job would be complete without the lint roller. Seems like we use that quite a bit, always trying to get some fuzz off something!

WORDS OF WISDOM:

Be nice to everyone. You never know who may hire you someday. And have fun with your work. Stylists aren't curing cancer or saving the world;

we're just making it a more beautiful place. And every celeb is a four-year-old waiting for their day to shine, and our job is to give that to them. The looks that we are creating and the pictures we are making will be a part of pop culture history. Years from now when historians look back on these times, hopefully a few of these moments will make the cut: Halle's Oscar dress, Salma [Hayek] in the tiara, Jada [Pinkett Smith] in the green cutoff Versace. These magazines, these photos, these images live on after a celeb is gone, and we are the creators of their image. The work we do is how they will be remembered. Not to mention the juicy stories that we tell about them later. Ooops! And finally, my last bit of advice that I always give assistants: Ask yourself, if Grace Kelly were a movie star today, would she wear this?

The anatomy of Phillip Bloch's prop kit

Q&A WITH TAYLOR JACOBSON

Taylor Jacobson, she of The Rachel Zoe Project *fame, shares a little about how she ended up the one everyone loved to hate on the Bravo show. She may have had an attitude, but the girl got things done. And that's what matters most.*

HOW DID YOU GET INTO THE STYLING BUSINESS?

Through a family friend—she's an amazing costume designer and I assisted the wardrobe department on some of her films. One thing led to another and I fell down the rabbit hole into the styling world.

WHO DID YOU WORK FOR FIRST?

Jessica Paster, Debra Waknin, and Andrea Lieberman.

HOW DID YOU MAKE YOUR WAY OVER TO RACHEL ZOE? DID YOU NEED TO PUSH ANYONE DOWN A FLIGHT OF STAIRS OR DID YOU JUST INTERVIEW LIKE EVERYONE ELSE?

I basically told everyone I wanted to work for her. I mean everyone! Doctors, friends, anyone who would listen. Eventually a position opened and it was a match made in heaven.

WERE YOU SUPER CONFIDENT WHEN YOU WALKED IN?

Yes, because I was determined to get the job!

WHAT IS THE MOST IMPORTANT THING TO KNOW ABOUT GETTING INTO THE FIELD?

Aspiring stylists need to know that styling is sooooo not glamorous. And you need to be devoted 100 percent—no matter!

BEST STYLING SECRET?

Undergarments are key.

NEIMANS, BARNEYS, OR SAKS—WHO HAS THE BEST SERVICES?

Loooooove Barneys!

WHAT'S YOUR FAVORITE LOOK WHEN YOU'RE SCHLEPPING FROM APPOINTMENT TO APPOINTMENT?

Black jeans, T-shirt, and a Chanel jacket.

BUDGETS

How much does it cost to dress a celebrity? Who pays for what? And more important, how much can you expect to make?

All jobs are different, but for the big-ticket assignments, the movie studios pay to dress the celebrities for junkets and premieres. Normally, there is a clause in the agreement that the budget will increase if the celeb gets nominated for an award (Oscar, Golden Globe, Grammy, SAG, etc.). In cases where a celebrity has two films up for awards, both studios will split the costs. She'll then need to be dressed for about eight red carpet appearances that require more formal attire and ten days of press and television appearances.

If this is a big star, the stylist will be looking at a total budget of around $35,000 to $40,000, plus an additional $15,000 for the awards show. This budget includes the stylist's fee with an assistant. Designers will usually give the celebrity the gown for the awards show, but the slightly less formal clothing for appearances, premieres, and junkets are usually purchased by the celebrity, along with all the underpinnings and accessories.

A celebrity stylist can expect to make $1,000 to $6,500 or more a day after everyone else is paid out of the budget. Your assignment will likely include one prep day, one day of shooting, and one day of returning. This schedule is typical for red carpet events that are not linked to a movie or press junket, or for some on-the-street looks. Meaning: Every time a client leaves the house, he or she is styled from head to toe. The average agency fee is $6,000 and the cost of a stylist's assistant is $900.

When you're on a magazine editorial shoot, you'll mostly borrow clothing in exchange for editorial credit in the magazine. You will also have a situation where you collaborate with a magazine's style director or stylist. So you will still get your day rates, plus prep and assistants, but you will be asked to combine your clothing (which can consist of six large roller bags) with whatever the magazine needs. You may get paid by the magazine or by the celebrity who wants you there. Celebrity stylist Phillip Bloch has said that he brings fifty to a hundred dresses to a fitting. Some dresses are borrowed, some bought, depending on the body and size of the celebrity.

Tailor: $1,500 on the low end. You *must* hire a tailor (see Tailor Made, page 139). Dresses you borrow from designers must be reworked for an actress with a smaller or wider frame. In addition, you may want the looks shortened, or armholes, necklines, and darts added, deleted, or replaced.

Suits need arms evened out or shoulders taken in. You may even need a complete reworking of a garment. Most times the budget includes the tailor. The exception is for magazine styling—very rarely will you need to hire a tailor because everything is shot from one angle and the clothing can be pinned or clamped from the back. But sometimes— depending on your idea, the celebrity, or situation—the magazine will spring for a tailor just to make the clothing work on a celebrity. This seems to happen more and more. (In the past, most editors were trained to do tailoring on the spot.)

Shoes: $750 (if they are bought).

Hair and makeup: $2,500 to $5,000 depending on the artist.

Jewelry: $750,000 to really make the look, and sometimes that comes with a bodyguard. Nearly all gems are borrowed. The actress is expected to say the name of the jewelry designer as free publicity in exchange for getting to borrow the bling.

Everything else: There are lots of hidden costs in dressing a celebrity. Keep in mind a stylist needs to budget for cell phone bills, messengers, garment bags, transportation, and miscellaneous expenditures. It adds up!

After all the pageantry is over, the dress designer either gives the celebrity the dress as a gift or it's given to charity. Elizabeth Saltzman, who styles Gwyneth Paltrow, told me that Paltrow has kept every single dress (except the pink Ralph Lauren, which is missing) archived and preserved for Apple Martin, her daughter. As well as all the accessories. What a lucky girl!

A FINAL NOTE

I've done my best here to give you an overview of how to pull a look together. There's a lot to remember and a lot to juggle. But the most important thing is to keep your mind open and find good people to work with. Take suggestions from tailors who have been doing all of this a lot longer than you, find a collaborator or a mentor, meet as many people as you can in the market, and study the clothing. Last, remember it's only a frock. Styling is hard work, but try to enjoy the beauty in it. It's supposed to be fun too!

Q & A WITH NEIL LANE

The king of reality-TV bling is Neil Lane. He's also a fine jeweler to elite actresses in Hollywood. Lane started designing jewelry while studying art at L'École des Beaux Arts in Paris in the 1970s. He had a great eye for collecting estate and vintage pieces of fine jewelry from Paris flea markets, where his passion for fine stones was born. He moved to Los Angeles, and soon his clients ranged from Barbra Streisand to Julia Roberts to Reese Witherspoon.

HOW DID YOU GET YOUR START IN JEWELRY DESIGN?

I started drawing things. I had little samples I found or collected. I would take these beautiful stones and try to make a design for them. I, myself, am not a platinum maker. I, myself, am not a jeweler. So it took me a while to find a craftsperson who could interpret my designs into a pretty ring. It was a lot of trial and error. My vision wasn't coming across the way I wanted. After a time, I met some great craftspeople, and the rings started coming out beautiful. I went from rings to diamond chains. When I came to Hollywood around 1989, there was no red carpet. There was no glamour. There was no Kate Hudson. Red carpet looks were black Armani suits with maybe a pair of diamond studs and maybe a little diamond bracelet and maybe a diamond pin on the lapel. That was considered glamour.

WHAT GOT YOU STARTED IN L.A.?

So I moved out to L.A. with a little bag of jewelry and set up a little shop. And I started to meet some cool people, some Hollywood people. My first clients were Barbra Streisand and Goldie Hawn and all their friends. Kate Hudson used to come into the store with her mother when she was a kid.

WEREN'T YOU WORKING FIRST WITH STYLISTS PHILLIP BLOCH AND DEBORAH WAKNIN?

Yes, both of them. I don't know how they found me. I didn't know anything about loaning jewelry. When red carpets started to get glamorous, stars were borrowing from Harry Winston—he was the guy. Somehow, I was getting young clients and the young movie stars. They would ask, "Neil, would you loan us that? Come on, we'd love to have a chain." So I started loaning out chains and other things that were useful. I remember the first time that Ellen Barkin said my name on one of those E! shows. My mother called me up. Renée Zellweger shouted my name. It was amazing to get the credit.

DO YOU THINK THAT WHEN WOMEN SEE THE ENTIRE LOOK TOGETHER IT BECOMES SOMETHING THAT'S INSPIRATIONAL, ASPIRATIONAL?

I think it becomes everything. Now with the Internet, looks are instantaneous. Women want to know what dress and what jeweler and what handbag and what clutch bag and what shoe. Everyone's part of the act. It's not even the celebrity anymore—it's just the image.

[Magazines must have had] to get magnifying glasses to find out where [a piece of] jewelry came from. I didn't know how the hell the magazines knew it was me. I didn't have P.R. people then. From my vantage point, it's been phenomenal and so fun. There's so much anxiety involved, but I'm here. And I do it 24/7. We used to do a red carpet once every couple of weeks. Now we do twenty a week.

WHAT DO YOU ENJOY MOST?

I really enjoy the personal relationships: Kate Bosworth, Renée, Angelina, having someone come in, or seeing a client at a party and giving her a hug. I enjoy relationships that've taken years to develop. I enjoy when an agent or a P.R. company calls to say that Megan Fox loved wearing Neil Lane at her premiere. You meet the girl and you're family and you're there for her and she's there for you. Being part of the fabric of it is emotionally satisfying in a human way.

AFTER THE AWARDS ARE DONE, ARE THE JEWELS RETURNED TO YOU OR ARE THEY SOMETIMES PURCHASED?

A lot of times they get bought. And not always by the celebrity. Sometimes it's someone who's seen it on them. When we put Angelina Jolie in a pair of our earrings for the cover of *People* in its Most Beautiful People issue, we thought, *Wow*. [But it didn't] translate to sales. [On the other hand,] when January Jones came in for the Emmys, we got a huge amount of attention. She wore a five-karat diamond and a beautiful bracelet—elegant. She loved the jewelry so much that her boyfriend bought something. She let us do these edgy great jewels, so we did some big colored diamond earrings and chains.

CHAPTER FOUR

Influencers, Icons, and Inspiration

It's amazing how a stylist can be inspired to create and produce a red carpet look based around a single object: a trench coat, a color of nail polish, a haircut. In my years in the business, I have compiled a huge assortment of photographs of objects and people who have influenced stylists, red carpet looks, videos, and trends. And you should too. The key is to keep your eyes open and absorb everything you can in all arenas—history, culture, fashion, art, and beauty.

Tara Swennen, who styles Kristen Stewart, told me: "One needs to work very hard to hone their abilities and stay ahead of the curve. I spend countless hours researching new ideas in movies, TV, advertising, books, et cetera. And then I take this inspiration and try to incorporate it into every look I put together. There is an art in that."

In this chapter, I've outlined the key fashion influencers and icons. That way, you'll know what it means when someone says, "The story is masculine/feminine, like Dietrich in the tuxedo," or "The whole shoot revolves around Ali MacGraw's crocheted *Love Story* hat," or "Bring me something that I haven't seen before but feels very *Belle de Jour*." Of course, there's no way to cover everything in this chapter. But these crib notes point you in the right direction.

REFERENCING: "I'M HAVING A _____ MOMENT"

As an assistant, you'll learn to develop a photographic memory for details, colors, dresses, iconic moments, events, and beautiful pictures. You need to keep current and know where you're going to find new material. Every time you work a job, you will need to bring something fresh to the table. You have to always anticipate what's coming next and forecast it like you're looking into a Magic 8 Ball or a daily horoscope.

One day my boss said to me, "I'm having a Jane Fonda in *Klute* moment." Huh? Who? WTF does that mean, exactly? I was dumbfounded when she referenced this movie star, film, and look and feel that I had no knowledge of.

Stylists are forever coming up with new spins on old ideas for a red carpet look or a shoot. So it pays to know your cultural references. Fashion people are always saying things like, "This is giving me Deneuve"—as in Catherine, the 1960s iconic French movie star and YSL muse—or "God, that's so completely *Grey Gardens*"—the documentary that inspires fashion magazines to do a story every two years on those two crazy Beale ladies (I think I called in clothing for about five *Grey Gardens*–like shoots!)—or "The line of the shoulder is so *Mildred Pierce*!"—the Joan Crawford movie that introduced furs and shoulder pads and ankle-strap shoes to the masses. This is called *referencing*—knowing where something comes from. It's giving the look an "aha" feel, putting the pieces together in such a way that they give a nod to an era, an icon, a movie, or a movement.

Referencing has to do with taking an old idea and finding new ways to spin it into a modern one. It's especially helpful to reference when you find yourself in a style slump, when you can't make head or tails of trends and fashion news or what to do with the clothes and accessories piled before you. How to get out of that slump? Reference.

Look at YouTube and old music videos. A huge majority of these songs were inspired by a movie or a photograph. Look at what Lady Gaga has referenced with her nine-minute "Telephone" video with Beyoncé. It is dinner and show—every possible pop/camp culture reference they

THE WHITE SUITS

Bianca Jagger, Heathrow
Airport, London, July 1972

George Harrison, Concert for
Bangladesh, New York, 1972

John Travolta, *Saturday Night Fever*, 1977

WHITE SUITS ARE INCREDIBLY POWERFUL. They don't just suggest confidence, knowledge, and sophistication—they create it! They do for the body what eyeglasses do for the face: make a person look intelligent and intriguing. Imagine how today's troubled stars would look in a perfectly tailored white suit: Lindsay Lohan, Heidi Spencer, or even Amy Winehouse would look completely transformed, egging us on to take them seriously. The white suit is a stylist's best friend.

Bianca Jagger was someone who was known mostly for her bohemian image, but once she strutted out in that infamous white suit we knew she was here to stay. She was letting us all know that she was a force to be reckoned with. Not only was she beautiful, but she was smart, in control, and all grown up.

When George Harrison busted out [a white suit] onstage, he broke out of the typical rocker mode; he went from follower to leader, from blending in to standing out, from boy to man.

I love young stars in white, because it creates a feeling of purity (there is a reason why brides wear it!). Britney always looked amazing in white, like the true star she is. Today we are overexposed to young girls overexposing themselves—after a while it just gets to be overwhelming and even gross. As stylists, we need to teach young starlets the value of pulling back and literally covering up sometimes. Wearing white is like wiping the slate clean.

I am a big believer in dressing respectfully when attending an event. If you're going to the Oscars or a Clive Davis party, you follow the code. When John Travolta donned that famous white suit on the disco dance floor in *Saturday Night Fever* it made an unforgettable statement. He was saying, "I respect myself, the club, and the art of dance itself." He was in total control—you couldn't take your eyes off him. As a stylist, I have always been aware of the set and make sure whoever I'm dressing pops off the scenery. When a wardrobe and set complement each other is when "moments" are created. John's white suit jumped off the screen at you from the sea of primary-colored boxes on the dance floor—pure genius! The white suits continue to pop off the red carpet to this day. —*Hayley Hill, former fashion director of* US Weekly, *founding editor of* Teen People, *and a celebrity stylist who has worked with Britney Spears, Justin Timberlake, Jessica Alba, Drew Barrymore, and Beyoncé*

could find, they threw in: Batman; *Caged Heat,* the 1974 women's prison movie; Quentin Tarantino movies; Russ Meyer's 1965 cult classic *Faster, Pussycat! Kill! Kill!*; and the hyper-saturated color of a David LaChappelle photograph. Madonna's "Hung Up" video was inspired by the movie *Saturday Night Fever.* I could go on and on.

Research on your own to keep up with how stylists reference and drop names of movies and photographers to describe what inspires them. There are those who can create ideas from scratch, and then there are people who just love to find great old images that are fun to riff on—to make people aware of the magic that once was. No one can do this for you. Go to the bookstore and cruise the fashion and style sections for old photographs. A particularly valuable resource is *Dressed: A Century of Hollywood Costume Design,* written by Deborah Nadoolman Landis (married to film director John Landis). It's filled with amazing movie photos and deep-inside-fashion information and inspiration.

Rent *All About Eve* to see how show business works and the amazing wardrobe Bette Davis wears. Watch *The Eyes of Laura Mars* with Faye Dunaway to see amazing graphic fashion photography, hear great music, and view incredible wardrobes. And, of course, memorize *Valley of the Dolls.* It seems that every couple of years, someone finds a still shot from this movie and decides to base an entire fashion advertising campaign on it, launching inspiration in fashion editorials, on the runway, and to the tips of your toes in pastel nail color.

It's also important to look at magazines. I had the great fortune to discuss influence and iconic imagery with Grace Mirabella, who started at *Vogue* in the 1950s, becoming its editor in chief from 1971 to 1988, then later serving as creator and editor at *Mirabella.* The time she served at these magazines left deep impressions on me and on other stylists. I asked her how aspiring stylists can learn from magazines. She said: "I think it's very important for the stylist to refer to the personality pages in the *Vogue* issues from the 1920s forward. These pages are key. They were not fashion pages but photographs and text about the arts—about stars performing onstage and, eventually, actresses in films. These stars were dressed in terrific blouses, superb necklines, even a raincoat. The screen actresses were photographed by superb, world-renowned photographers. These were not fashion pictures. They were often pictures of fine talent. The pictures suggested the personality's style, her own or the role she was playing, and, without question, we at *Vogue* preferred looks that were alluring and real, not artificial. We never exaggerated these pictures. The clothes were not jokes, not extravaganza, more the personality's style.

"The fashion pictures were different but," continued Mirabella, "in my years, they were appealing, often amusing, sometimes erotic, and sometimes extreme. During my period as editor in chief at *Vogue,* the photographs and the star were more relaxed—the clothes more relaxed. 'Celebrity' didn't carry weight until the late '80s. Without question, we preferred looks that were sensuous and real—not artificial."

DECADE CRAWL

It's essential to know your history, decades, and the key players. You should know that Cleopatra was actually a real queen of Egypt (circa 69 B.C.–30 B.C.) . . . and not Elizabeth Taylor; that a Josephine-style empire dress is attributed to Joséphine de Beauharnais, wife of Napoleon Bonaparte in the late 1700s. Get educated on key designers such as Yves Saint Laurent and Halston (not Sarah Jessica Parker, who is CEO and president of Halston Heritage, but the *real* Halston) and Coco Chanel (*not* Karl Lagerfeld, who is the creative director); photographers like Helmut Newton, Chris von Wangenheim, Guy Bourdin, and Herb Ritts; actresses; and musicians.

When we look at style now, it all seems to have some origin in the past. For instance, stylist Rachel Zoe's girls, as well as Zoe herself, love to dress like free-spirited California girls with a huge nod to 1970s maxi dresses, platform shoes, oversize sunglasses, and long flowing hair.

It's important to know your history. You should know the designers who started a bandage dress craze (Azzedine Alaïa in 1980, followed by Hervé Léger in 1985, and Max Azria, who bought and designs the label Hervé Léger today). Research the origins of grunge and what this look is (Seattle, 1980s); know who invented the miniskirt (Mary Quant, 1960s). Get a grip on the mood of the time and the emotional state of your country and the world. Notice how everything has a tendency to go "in" and then back "out" and overlap. You'll see that even Lady Gaga has built her image by referencing what means most to her and her music.

SHOW AND TELL

Here is a compilation of photographs of people who moved and rocked and shook our world. Pictures that bring a sigh. Some with drop-dead outfits that instantly make you recall something you've just seen on the red carpet or on the rail at Curve L.A., or that generally make you think about how you can build an idea around an iconic picture.

The Graduate

"Anne Bancroft in *The Graduate* [1967] did a lot for women of a certain age. She was the first ever cougar. She defined

Anne Bancroft in *The Graduate*, 1967

Q & A WITH ROBERT VERDI

Robert Verdi is not only Eva Longoria's right-hand man when it comes to getting dressed, but he's a reality star in his own right, having starred in his very own eponymous show.

WHO ARE THE KEY PLAYERS TO REFERENCE? WHO SHOULD ASPIRING STYLISTS LOOK AT?

The Olsen sisters. You should also know Cher, Veronica Lake, Shirley MacLaine in her early years when she had the little pixie cut, Brigitte Bardot, Marilyn Monroe, Audrey Hepburn, Grace Kelly. And the model Penelope Tree—she's an important one for people to know. She's a watershed moment because she captured a defining moment in fashion history. She was photographed by Richard Avedon when I think she was seventeen. She's this glamorous rocker, and there's something androgynous about her at the same time. She's irreverent and incredibly stylish. She was kind of accessible and yet incredibly inspirational. She's such a good balance. She's incredibly unique in her image. I just love her. But you have to make the references modern. You start with a reference that puts the look in context, and then you think, "This girl in today's times."

WHO'S THE MOST IMPORTANT FASHION DESIGNER?

I still say Chanel because she's the most referenced one. Valentino, Yves Saint Laurent, Ralph Lauren, Bill Blass. Today, one of the most important American designers, and certainly not because of the *Project Runway* success, is Michael Kors. He's come to understand the seamless life that women today live, which is going day to night and from work to weekend, wanting to feel sophisticated, comfortable, casual, and dressed-up enough. It's comfortable but fashion forward, and I think he gets it. So that makes him one of the most important designers right now. When I put one of his dresses on Eva [Longoria] or Kathy Griffin, I never go wrong.

WHAT'S YOUR FAVORITE EVA LONGORIA LOOK THAT YOU'VE STYLED?

This past year at the Cannes Film Festival in a blue Versace dress. There are some distant shots of her on the red carpet where she's not even facing the camera. There's nobody else on the carpet but her. There's thousands of photographers and she's just standing there, floating. I love that photo.

WAS SHE YOUR FIRST CLIENT?

Yeah, she was. I had done styling before, but nobody had hired me to put their wardrobe together for their life and public image. She just trusted me. We have the same instincts. We both like color. We both like shine.

NOW YOU HAVE OTHER CELEBRITY CLIENTS. HOW DO YOU HANDLE THEIR OPINIONS?

I've set up a relationship with all my clients whereby they respect me as the expert. That's true in all professional situations. If you walk into a doctor's office, you understand that the doctor has an expertise that you don't have. You may ask questions. But the questions are never going to counter his professional opinion. Stylists have an area of expertise.

HOW DO YOU CREATE A STRONG IMAGE FOR CELEBRITIES?

The perception the public has of celebrities is built through a series of images. The number of images you see of celebrities outnumbers the number of words you hear from them. That's why stylists create these images for them. It's to sort of build a brand and a public image.

So what we are, in many ways, are social psychologists. For example, if Eva were going to the Emmys but was not nominated while everybody else in the cast was nominated, you can't put her in head-to-toe beads in a scene-stealing dress. You have to be respectful of the situation. But if your client is nominated for an Oscar, the Oscar nominees always wear the most over-the-top, couture, extravagant gowns. That's appropriate. It's all about context.

HOW IMPORTANT IS THAT PICTURE OF THE CELEBRITY IN THE DESIGNER DRESS WHEN IT GETS BROADCAST?

It is incredibly important. These are the images that help build their careers, that bring them fashion contracts and invitations to certain events internationally. It makes them a fashion authority and therefore makes them money. You're helping create a public image that's creating a revenue stream.

WHAT DO YOU LOVE MOST ABOUT WHAT YOU DO?

That styling allows me to tell a story. When you're dressing somebody, you're telling a story to the world that could potentially live on forever as a moment in history, like Jennifer Lopez and the Versace dress. I think that's what a stylist hopes to achieve: an incredible moment that's captured.

WHAT PART OF STYLING DON'T YOU LIKE?

Feeling rejected if you ask for something and you don't get it. Or you organize things and the timing is all off. I've had situations where I worked really hard, but the timing was just off and the dress got there too late and it didn't get worn. It's a reputation business. A designer will think, "I let him borrow all the time, and his client never wears anything I lend. He can't get a client into anything." It can turn into that too. Your reputation's always at risk.

Mildred Pierce, Joan Crawford, 1945

Ann-Margret and Elvis in *Viva Las Vegas*, 1964

a new kind of youthful thinking in dressing that wasn't too young but refused to give in to old. She's a woman really in her prime who doesn't look dowdy, who is unabashedly sexy." —*Isaac Mizrahi, designer*

Mildred Pierce

"Joan Crawford in *Mildred Pierce* [1945] changed everyone's eye at the time with her clothes and styling in that movie. Her shoulders were bigger, her eyebrows bolder, her hair rattier than anyone had seen at that point. [Her look] had a graphic quality about it, and people thought it was a bit caricature. It wasn't till a little later that all that aggressive bold attire became really chic in a broad way." —*Isaac Mizrahi*

Viva Las Vegas

"Ann-Margret in *Viva Las Vegas* [1964] walked the exact border between trashy and prim. She was a girl who could go to the edge in tight hot pants and high heels and yet not go over the border into bad-girl. She was bad-girl enough but always came back to being good-girl." —*Hayley Hill*

Diane Keaton in *Annie Hall*, 1977

Linda Evans and Joan Collins, *Dynasty*, 1981

Annie Hall

"The late '70s were all about modernizing womenswear with masculine elements. Similar to how Marlene Dietrich wore the tuxedo in the 1930s, the '70s saw Diane Keaton appropriating menswear with khakis, a vest, and a rolled-up white shirt in *Annie Hall*. Ralph Lauren designed the clothes and fabrics, taking WASPY dressing and creating a street chic look. Ruth Morley, the costume designer, put it all together in an unforgettable way." —*Cameron Silver, owner of Decades boutiques in Los Angeles and London*

Dynasty

"Just like we say *Kleenex* for *tissue* and *Nikes* for *sneakers,* the very word *Dynasty* is synonomous with *rich,* and the wardrobe should get all the credit! From over-the-top metallic fabrics to the oversize Texas-style jewelry, these legendary looks will long outlast the show [1980s], because who doesn't want to be rich?" —*Hayley Hill*

Barbara Parkins, Sharon Tate, and Patty Duke in *Valley of the Dolls*, 1967

Christina Hendricks in *Mad Men*, 2007

Valley of the Dolls

"*Valley of the Dolls* [1967] brought the psychedelic sub-culture to the mainstream. Travilla's costume designs launched the baby-doll dress into popularity. Sharon Tate was the quintessential beauty of the late 1960s, and in this look we see her in the vibrancy of prints of that era." —*Cameron Silver*

Christina Hendricks, *Mad Men*

"Whether covered up or strategically displayed, Christina Hendricks's hard-to-ignore curves remind us of the type of female figure worshiped decades ago. Her perfect hour-glass shape implies a feminine power that she is not afraid of or trying to hide. It is both refreshing and inspiring to see a contemporary actress embrace her curves in such an unapologetic way, especially considering the ultra skinny body du-jour in Hollywood today." —*Hayley Hill*

Gia Carangi getting tattooed

Photographer Chris von Wangenheim

"Chris von Wangenheim was a disciple and close friend of Helmut Newton. Chris's women were softer and more vulnerable than Helmut's. He was a true collaborator. He always brought his team into the plotting and he would really listen. He was very demanding and his shoots often ended up being quite costly. I remember a particularly costly shoot. We were out West, and he was looking for a dried river or lakebed. After a day of scouting we still hadn't found the right one. So he ended up hiring a helicopter to scout with, and then ultimately used it in the photos. He always got the shot. That was all that mattered to him." —*Jade Hobson, former creative director of* Vogue *and* Mirabella

Herb Ritts, "Naomi, seated," 1991

Jennifer Beals, *Flashdance*, 1983

Herb Ritts

"What I loved about Herb's approach to photography is that it was always organic—he loved all the forms and textures of nature. Through his lens he was always searching for all that was strange and odd. He immersed his models in sand, water, trees, and mud so that they would become part of the landscape, and something magical would happen. That is why he loved to use nudity a lot and natural daylight.

"It was always extraordinary when we worked together, as something new and strange would evolve out of our stories. We were lucky to be able to explore and take risks in those days back then, as magazines like British *Vogue* had not been over-commercialized." —*Sarajane Hoare, stylist who worked with Ritts*

Flashdance

"*Flashdance* came out in 1983, before people were wearing sweats as everyday wear. This was Juicy Couture before Juicy Couture. Michael Kaplan, the costume designer, created a look that celebrated both fitness and a woman's body. It was how dancers dressed in the studio. Jennifer Beals in a leotard, legwarmers, and sweatshirt falling off her shoulders influenced how everyone else wanted to dress in the '80s." —*Cameron Silver*

Faye Dunaway in *Bonnie and Clyde*, 1967

Stevie Nicks, 1970

Grace Kelly in *Rear Window*, 1954

Bonnie and Clyde

"This is a great look that Theodora van Runkle created for the movie in 1967. The silhouette is like a skyscraper. Almost any body type can pull this look off. The costumes in *Bonnie and Clyde* were so youthful—architectural in a way that's not fussy. They were gorgeous but did not distract from the movie characters." —*Doris Raymond, owner, the Way We Wore, Los Angeles*

Stevie Nicks

"Stevie is one of the first people I styled. She's amazing. When we first talked, she had clear ideas of what she wanted to do. She wanted to project kind of an ethereal spirited person. She's so tiny and waif-like that we decided to use diaphanous, light, airy things that would transform with the lights. That way she could appear very, very big in 'Rhiannon' and very diminutive in 'Sarah.' The aim was that the audience would see the movement and the vibe change.

She did wardrobe changes very sparingly at first, so the costumes needed to do a lot of work. She really respects fine fabrics and the quality, the integrity of the garments. She has the originals of the first things I ever did for her. I'm talking about beautiful and beaded chantilly laces, silk, chiffon, georgettes, silk-cut velvets, cob-web beaded lace. They're sensual. The silhouettes are really quite basic. They're engineered to move beautifully." —*Margi Kent, Stevie Nicks' stylist*

Rear Window

"Who doesn't want to look like Grace Kelly—especially in this costume created by Edith Head? She is probably the most referenced woman. She's the minimalist of the '50s. Minimalism is always classic because it's totally timeless and ageless. It's just about not trying too hard. It's about inner beauty." —*Cameron Silver*

Audrey Hepburn in *Funny Face*, 1957

Jackie Onassis, New York, October 7, 1971

Funny Face

"Audrey Hepburn was so influential with her looks. She was the perfect muse that all the costume designers wanted to dress. This look is by Edith Head for *Funny Face* in 1957. The way clothing skimmed her body showed her gamine physique in a way that was tasteful and seductive at the same time. She was elegant in the way that Jackie O. was." —*Doris Raymond*

Jackie Onassis, 1971

"Jackie Onassis exemplified classic New York uptown chic in this paparazzi image, providing proof to generations of women to come that femininity can be achieved in a well-fitted pair of pants and simple sweater. It's inspirational because there's mystery and aura to the look, not to mention a confidence that was well ahead of its time. Influential because she, along with Katharine Hepburn, forever ingrained in fashion the notion of menswear tailoring." —*Jim Shi, New York City–based fashion and lifestyle journalist who has covered the international fashion circuit from New York and London to Milan and Paris*

Jean Harlow in *Dinner at Eight*, 1933

Ali MacGraw, 1971

Dinner at 8

"This picture is proof that a dress—in this case by Adrian, who costumed all of MGM's leading ladies throughout much of the 1930s and 1940s—can make a woman. Jean Harlow was little known before this Depression-era film where she played Kitty, the original, original desperate housewife. This dress brought a sense of fantasy and dreaminess to millions of women (not to mention making it acceptable to wear a gown that matches one's hair color). In the troubled times of the early '30s, Harlow's form-fitting white satin evening gown with fluffy shoulders and bare back gave women their femininity back." —*Jim Shi*

Ali MacGraw, 1971

"Ali MacGraw is an East Coast, well-bred girl. In this shot her face looks completely natural, with no makeup and a heavy eyebrow. Everything she's wearing is well made. It's still hippie and bohemian, but the quality pieces make her look well bred." —*Paul Cavaco,* Allure *magazine's creative director*

Kate Moss, Heathrow Airport, 2008

Grace Jones, London, October, 1981

Kate Moss, 2008

"Kate is the master of mixing pieces to achieve a unique look. She's always playing with proportion and style. She'll mix a little glamour with a little bohemian. She can mix all sorts of elements from high and low and from different eras, yet somehow retains her own individual look. She never looks costumey because she manages to always do something personal with her ensembles. It's how she mixes it together." —*Paul Cavaco*

Grace Jones, 1981

"There's a dangerousness to her look. Grace personifies the disco era, which was sexy and a little dark. It was about clubs, nightlife, and music, and Grace embodies that era." —*Paul Cavaco*

Madonna, New York, 1984

Debbie Harry, 1981

Madonna, 1984

"This look spoke to a lot of young girls across the country because it was an easily duplicated look. It wasn't too tortured and complicated. It wasn't like you had to blow out your hair. You didn't have to do a lot of things to emulate this look. You didn't have to spend a lot of money to get to it. Her look here had a rebellious nature to it. She wasn't skinny, skinny, skinny or built up then. She had a girl's body, which helped her style look completely attainable." —*Annie Ladino, a New York-based stylist, fashion editor, author, and current contributor to* Elle *magazine*

Debbie Harry, 1981

"Debbie Harry is the true pioneer of the club kid movement. To this day we see her influence in modern pop stars like Gwen Stefani and Madonna. Her understated sexiness and force captivated audiences [then] and still does today." —*Annie Ladino*

Q&A WITH LADY STARLIGHT

Lady Starlight knows Stefani Joanne Angelina Germanotta better than almost anyone. She helped create the genius that is the Lady Gaga aesthetic, which really isn't surprising seeing that she's been creating performance art since age seven.

WHAT WERE YOUR EARLY MUSIC INFLUENCES?

The first bands that had major impact on me were the Stray Cats and the Monkees. I always had an attraction to music and fashion from earlier eras. I can definitely attribute my first fashion risk to my passion for the Monkees. I was inspired by Mike Nesmith to wear my dad's Frye boots to school in 5th grade! They totally didn't fit, but I was compelled to express my excitement about the music . . . I guess I have been doing this ever since.

WHAT WAS YOUR FIRST ORIGINAL DESIGN OR LOOK?

My brother and I later had a band called Enter-In. I "styled" the band. Our look was bed sheets over our heads with torn pieces of paper taped to our faces scrawled with nonsensical text. Hahaha, maybe I'll revisit this look!

ARE YOU MORE INTERESTED IN SPECIFIC LOOKS OR SPECIFIC DESIGNERS?

Most definitely specific looks! Designers don't interest me at all. I approach fashion from a socio-cultural perspective. I'm interested in what individuals have to say with their fashion choices. Fashion is the ultimate form of non-verbal communication. This is pretty obvious with sub-cultural fashion (which is my major area of interest), but *everyone* says something with his or her clothes, even no statement is a statement.

DO YOU CONSIDER YOURSELF A STYLIST, PERSONAL SHOPPER, RETAIL THERAPIST, OR A STYLE ARCHITECT?

I'm probably most accurately described as a style mentor. I get a sense of individuals and give them the tools they need to fulfill their style potential. I give them historical references. Having this knowledge is what will ultimately set the person apart from the crowd. It radiates from within.

DESCRIBE YOUR DESIGN PROCESS.

It's quite simple really: I see what I want something to look like in my head and if it doesn't exist, I make it exist.

DESCRIBE YOUR INFLUENCES.

Music fuels all my creative output. My looks reflect the music I'm passionate about at the time. During the early 2000s, I was obsessed with '60s freak beat and UK psych—Small Faces, Pretty Things, The Creation, The Action, and more obscure stuff like The Syn and Q'65. I expressed this obsession by appropriating the look of the ultimate icon of the era, Peggy Moffitt. Next came my obsession with '70s Glam—Bowie, T-Rex, Roxy, Gary Glitter, Wizzard, Alvin Stardust, Sparks. . . . What better way to express this obsession than with the Ziggy Stardust look. Next up were Iron Maiden and the NWOBHM scene. It was all about denim, leather studs, and spandex. Girlschool was a big influence on my look. Now I'm deep into prog, Rush, [Pink] Floyd, Van der Graaf, and Hawkwind.

WHEN YOU FIRST SAW LADY GAGA WHAT DID YOU THINK? WHAT DID YOU WANT TO ENHANCE OR STRIP AWAY?

She definitely had a great look already, but it was not as flamboyant as I thought it should be. She was in the music business from a young age, so she was surrounded by the boring, uncreative

Lady Gaga and Lady Starlight, 2008

people in the industry. When we started working together and became friends, I gave her my insight and encouragement to just go for it.

WHAT LOOKS DO YOU FORECAST FOR THE NEAR FUTURE?

A return to Earth is inevitable. The futuristic, plasticine image that GaGa has made a trend can only be followed by the opposite. Warm, rich, earthy, relatable style, and personas will rule. I'm looking at Dark Side–era Pink Floyd and 2112 era Rush for inspiration at the moment . . . it's all about '70s Arena Rock looks for me.

Courtney Love, Reading Rock Festival, England, 1994

Cher, August 1971

Diana Ross, *Mahogany*, 1975

Courtney Love, 1994

"Courtney Love is known as the Princess of Grunge because she took her look from grunge to glam. In the early '90s she had alternative girls everywhere running to get baby doll dresses and combat boots. Her feisty and rebellious attitude shows through even when she's rocking a slinky gown and red lips." —*Annie Ladino*

Cher, 1971

"Cher leaves us nostalgic for the '70s. She's fearless and carefree. She dressed like a hippie even before the term was coined and introduced us to a nontailored, unrigged way of dressing." —*Annie Ladino*

Mahogany

"Diana Ross is the fashion diva defined. A constant fashion chameleon, she's never afraid to take risks and has been pushing the fashion envelope since her days in The Supremes. In *Mahogany*, she reached her diva pinnacle. Most people don't know she designed many of those iconic *Mahogany* costumes herself. Not only was she a talented stylist and designer in her own right, but she was a champion of African American style. She brought high fashion into the music world, and created the unique, elegant, singular Diana Ross style that still influences designers and stylists today." —*Rob Zangardi, a stylist who has worked with Rihanna, Ciara, Jeremy Piven, Rachel McAdams, Will Smith, and Kerry Washington*

Lauren Hutton, 1970

Liza Minelli, *Cabaret*, 1972

Lauren Hutton, 1970

"What makes Lauren Hutton so inspiring is her timeless-ness. It was unheard of to hire a model with a gap between her teeth back when Lauren was discovered, but she had something special—and it has lasted for decades. This '70s menswear-inspired outfit is very classic with clean lines. It reminds me of the way Lauren liked to dress in real life. Her spirit, her look, and the way she dresses has inspired many fashion shoots." *—Ann Caruso, a stylist who's worked with Padma Lakshmi, Katherine Heigl, Christina Applegate, Claire Danes, Drew Barrymore, and many more. She's also worked as a contributing editor for* Harper's Bazaar, InStyle, Town and Country, Oprah, *and* Vanity Fair

Liza Minelli/*Cabaret*, 1972

"Liza's look in *Cabaret* has had such a strong influence in fashion and art. This image is so striking. Her hair, makeup (the red lips and the lashes with the bright shadow), the hat, the stockings, and deep v-neck of her top made a memo-rable statement that we've seen reinterpreted over and over. Fashion likes to repeat and reinterpret itself by enjoying the moment all over again—especially when the style state-ments are timeless, like this one." *—Ann Caruso*

Jimi Hendrix

"Jimi's style has inspired fashion designers, celebrities, and stylists for decades. He was a true original, mixing bohe-mian, dandy, military, western, and rock styles with iconic pieces like the band leader jacket he made famous. You can still see his influence in everything from Balmain, Gucci, and Stella McCartney collections to the styles of Kate Moss, Kanye West, Nicole Richie, and Beyonce." *—Rob Zangardi*

Jimi Hendrix, 1967

Brigitte Bardot, 1961

Victoria Beckham, New York, June 14, 2007   Mariah Carey, New York, June 7, 2007   Naomi Campbell, Munich, July 10, 2007

Brigitte Bardot, 1961

"What I love about this photo of Brigitte Bardot is that it feels so candid. For a stylist, it's so important to have a sense of the history of fashion—to understand how a fashion icon is created and placed in history. We stylists today borrow ideas from and become inspired by these legendary icons. To be a stylist, you must study fashion history books, old magazines, and watch old movies. Stylists draw, shape, and mold the styles of today from these historical references. I know exactly what my client means when she says, 'I want the look to feel Brigitte Bardot.' Ms. Bardot provides fantastic inspiration for today's image-makers. Her look is current and relevant . . . beautiful and sexy." —*Trish Townsend, Carrie Underwood's stylist*

Azzedine Alaïa, Designer, June and July 2007

"Azzedine Alaïa has made a very specific contribution to fashion: he was the first person to take sex and make it chic. Before Azzedine, fashion was devoid of overt sexuality. The world of fashion always kept sex at arm's length: sex was tacky. Sex was Frederick's of Hollywood. Sex was cheesy. Sex was the opposite of Chanel. Chic women would never dress in an overtly sexual way. And then, in the early '80s, Azzedine arrived. Azzedine created sexy, alluring clothing which was so sophisticated that it was impossible to see it as anything other than chic. He created clothing which was executed at the highest level. His fabric, his cutting, and his marriage of technology and craft allowed him to inject the world of fashion with a high-class, unimpeachably chic eroticism. Our culture is now so saturated with the idea of sexiness and 'hotness' that it is hard to tell the difference between cheap hoochie-style and real style. If you want a lesson in couture allure, then go check out the rack of Azzedine Alaïa at your local Barneys. He's still the best." —*Simon Doonan, creative director of Barneys New York*

CHAPTER FIVE

Personal Style and New Image

I am absolutely bananas over the way Sienna Miller transforms her look from week to week; how Victoria Beckham morphed from a Spice Girl into a successful fashion designer and stylish mother; and how Nicole Richie has made herself over from a party girl and Paris Hilton sidekick to a style icon in just a few short years. It's not easy to reinvent your style—especially in the public eye. I've witnessed many missteps along the way. But, with a stylist's help, anyone can make an awe-inspiring transition.

Everyone's style needs to evolve over time. When celebrities have a style rebirth in front of the world it can be pretty scary. Some are masters of switching it up and keeping us guessing. Carrie Underwood, Sarah Jessica Parker, and Rihanna are a few of my favorites. Others try to change their look, but they can't quite pull it off because they rely too much on outside opinions, gimmicky trends, and occasionally the wrong stylist.

At *Harper's Bazaar*, my boss was the late great Elizabeth Tilberis. She was responsible for styling the "girls" in the Robert Palmer video "Addicted to Love." She put them all in the same Azzedine Alaïa dresses with their hair pulled back severely, their makeup thick and black around the eyes, and their lips lacquered in red. She was also the editor who commissioned British *Vogue*'s black-and-white supermodel cover with Linda Evangelista, Christy Turlington, Naomi Campbell, Cindy Crawford, and Tatjana Patitz in 1990, which ushered in that new era of models not getting out of bed for less than $10,000 a day. The cream-of-the-crop stylists really can make the history books for defining a unique style.

One thing that always makes me insane is when a celebrity just buys in to a look that makes him or her look like a carbon copy of another actor. You see that a lot. Sometimes I can't tell one girl from the other, and this is a huge danger. It is important to maintain original style.

Madonna is the one celebrity who, after almost three decades, continues to succeed at reinventing herself and maintaining an individual style. She never fails to enthrall us with her new looks. She is a technician who knows how to light herself, how to pose, and how to seduce. She can go from total 1980s street urchin to Eva Perón to geisha and then to a single mother with a kickin' bod.

Madonna is on the extreme end of self-transformation. Many remakes are subtle and take place over time, which is key in Hollywood. You don't want magazines and the blogosphere making fun of your client because the change is so severe. Stylist Wayne Scot Lukas, who has styled Tina Turner and Janet Jackson, told me that "the best way to maintain a certain image while trying new things is to really get to know the client. Let the subtle style shifts happen gradually and don't incorporate anything too shocking."

I was lucky to get a take on image renewal and rebirth from Stacy London, who entertains us all with her expertise on the TLC show *What Not to Wear*, as well as being the Pantene brand ambassador, a *Today Show* contributor, and founding partner of Style for Hire. I also polled celebrity makeup artist Troy Surratt, who trained under makeup artist Kevyn Aucoin before launching his own mega-successful career. Surratt has worked with the likes of Charlize Theron,

Stacy Ferguson, Burbank, CA, February 2003

Fergie, Grammy Awards, Los Angeles, January 2010

Mary-Kate and Ashley Olsen, Jennifer Lopez, Hilary Swank, and Maggie Gyllenhaal.

Stacy London says: "The key to achieving great personal style is knowing that it isn't a static thing. Your style should evolve over a period of time as you age, become more and more knowledgeable about your own body shape, become aware of which trends work for you, and, let's face it, have more money to buy those fancy clothes. In terms of star style, it is important for celebrities to evolve in terms of their look without alienating their audience. Many women have successfully achieved this."

CELEBRITY TRANSFORMATIONS

Stacy London and Troy Surratt pored over pictures of celebs who have changed on the carpet throughout the years. Some have gone from over-the-top trendy to completely elegant and refined. In this chapter, we examine the changes and offer advice for guiding a client (or yourself) into new style territory. We call out what worked and what didn't quite work and explain how to make helpful suggestions when the time is right for change.

FERGIE

Fergie is a pop princess and member of the Black Eyed Peas. We've watched her go from a wild child to a sensual married woman. She has no fear of changing her hair color, clothing, and body.

"Fergie's transition has been a somewhat interesting one," says London. "While always a fan of tight, body-skimming clothing, she transformed her style from street to chic by 'growing it up'—in other words, removing the eyebrow piercing and skipping the sweatshirts and more urban hairstyles in favor of something softer. She went through a pinup, sex-symbol phase and has arrived at something more sophisticated and modern by darkening her hair, lightening up her makeup, and choosing pieces that, while flattering, are less overtly sexual, announcing her new film career and status as a married woman."

Surratt adds: "Fergie allows her self-expression to take place through her ever-changing hairstyles. Her makeup doesn't change as much, as she sticks with an emphasis on eyes, like upper lashes. Her lip look is nude to neutral. But with her hair she'll try anything and everything, from braids and cornrows to dying it brunette. While she is still very edgy, we've kind of watched Fergie grow up from a crazy club girl to a movie star in *Nine*—complete with a movie

Gwen Stefani of No Doubt, MTV Video Music Awards,
Los Angeles, September 1998

Gwen Stefani, NYC, October 2009

star husband. Her hair is a more natural tone, even when she's wearing it darker. While it's still very styled most of the time, it's not nearly as wacky as it once was, which is more appropriate for her age now."

GWEN STEFANI

This recording artist, fashion designer, and lead vocalist for the band No Doubt married Gavin Rossdale of the U.K. band Bush in 2002. In 2003, she debuted her fashion line L.A.M.B.; her solo album released in 2004; 2006 welcomed baby style icon Kingston James; and in 2008 she had her second boy, Zuma.

"Gwen Stefani's style evolution has always turned heads. At the start of her career the braces, blue hair, red lips, and outrageously revealing midriff clothing spoke to the rebelliousness and brashness with which she hit the music scene," Stacy London says. "As she developed her career as a solo artist, actress, and fashion designer, and then became a mom, her style began to transform. While trading in blue hair for platinum, Gwen's shock value may have dissipated, but it was replaced with the allure of a timeless Hollywood

screen siren. Like Jean Harlow, Kim Novak, and even Marilyn Monroe, Stefani's new style speaks to the classic blond femme fatale who is also just a little fragile. Trading in red lips for pale ones is an easy way to make a stylish transition from pop star to entrepreneur, from young ingenue to sophisticated celebrity."

Surratt adds: "One of the things about star style is that a celebrity's look can help brand him or her and make him or her as iconic as a Nike swoosh or a red can of Coke. Gwen's red lips are important and have mostly remained the same, while her eye makeup or hair color will change. She is committed to her red mouth, similar to the J.Lo glow that everyone has been trying to get for the past ten years. Gwen made a switch to a very, very pale lip for a period of time, and it also really worked for her. You just have to find that right tone that works for you, and then own it, wear it with confidence. The great thing is that after two babies and being a good wife to rocker Gavin Rossdale, she's still maintained her rock goddess image. That's really what Gwen does with every one of her beauty and style choices."

Q & A WITH CRISTINA EHRLICH

Cristina Ehrlich made a name for herself, along with her styling partner Estee Stanley, working with starlets like Jessica Biel, Penélope Cruz, and Elisha Cuthbert. She's one of the chicest people in the business.

DESCRIBE YOUR STYLING AESTHETIC.

The best way to describe what my overall objective continually is, regardless of the girl or event, is that the final product is always chic, classic, and timeless. Every woman has a different part of her body that makes her feel most confident and beautiful. Instead of trying to fit a woman to a trend, I fit the clothes to highlight the individual qualities of each of my clients.

WHAT INFLUENCE DO YOU THINK YOUR STYLING HAS HAD ON YOUNG WOMEN?

My point of view for each of my clients, regardless of age or size, is something individual but still timeless and effortless. I want every woman to develop her own sense of style and confidence. I consistently use European women as my inspiration.

WHAT DO YOU LOVE ABOUT WHAT YOU DO?

Everything. I love the artistic license that I am afforded as each job develops. Different projects require different clothes, and no two projects are the same. I love the relationships I build with each client; the one-on-one time we spend is both creative and collaborative. I love the process—the frenetic beginning of a project carried through to the rewarding end, when a woman finds the dress that makes her feel beautiful and confident.

WHAT ARE YOUR FAVORITE CRISTINA-STYLED RED CARPETS?

For Penélope Cruz, during her nomination for *Vicki Cristina Barcelona*, we had several red carpet moments with Azzedine Alaïa; during the 2007 Academy Awards, the beautiful pink Versace was stunning. [I'm also fond of] Amy Adams at the 2009 SAG Awards in the strapless gown by Giambattista Valli and Isabel Lucas in vintage Chanel at the L.A. premiere of *Transformers 2*.

Rihanna, Manchester, England, November 2006

MTV Video Music Awards, New York, August 2006

Nickelodeon Kids' Choice Awards, Los Angeles, March 2007

RIHANNA

Robyn Rihanna Fenty was born in 1988 and raised in Barbados. In a very short period of time, Rihanna's career skyrocketed, and in 2007, she became one of the biggest-selling female recording artists. Modeling contracts followed, and suddenly every single move she made was documented, obsessed over, and widely copied by her peers and millions of fans.

London says: "Rihanna's style evolution has been a brilliant one and an essential part of her success. While stunningly beautiful when arriving from Barbados, the long curly hair and *au naturel* look did not necessarily separate her from the pack.

"Her evolution took its first bold turn when she cut her hair into an asymmetric bob, signifying her desire to step out and embrace a more avant-garde style, one with more bravado.

"Since then, she has experimented with styles from the highest designers, looking for pieces that are on the edge of outrageous but simultaneously appealing. This style garners attention, gossip, and wonder. Add to the mix

the colored eye shadows, neon nails, and bright accessories, and one can see how Rihanna was destined to rise to the top of the music scene."

Surratt adds: "Watching Rihanna's evolution has been really fun. She was a bit of a good girl in the beginning. Maybe she was going for the go-to Beyoncé look. But now she's evolved into a style all her own. She's done the diagonal forward bob, the faux hawk pompadour. And her makeup look has become more creative—she has warm skin but experiments with cool tones. The natural inclination with warm, caramel skin is to stick to coppery brown shades. But she tends to create contrasts, like wearing purple or blue on her eyes, or a bright pink lip and really rosy cheeks. She plays a lot with lashes, which are instantly feminizing and add a femininity and flirtatiousness to the face. Rihanna makes bold color choices that are atypical and daring and often create contrast with her warm skin. It's great that she doesn't follow everyone's rules. She commands attention and keeps people guessing."

Costume Institute Gala, Metropolitan Museum of Art, New York, May 2009

Cannes, France, January 2010

Carrie Underwood, *American Idol* Finale, Hollywood, CA, May 2005

Billboard Music Awards at MGM Grand, Las Vegas, December 2005

CARRIE UNDERWOOD

This 2005 *American Idol* winner is a hugely successful country pop singer and songwriter who has won multiple Grammys. We noticed quite a morph when she graduated from *American Idol*. She grew up and into a more sophisticated look with each red carpet appearance. Surratt says: "Carrie is always blond with loads of lashes and golden skin. But she has totally evolved. Her hair has gotten softer and more modern. She's often quite coiffed—like so many Southern girls, she's no stranger to the can of hair spray. We first met her on *Idol*, and she was all about everything big: big hair and big voice. Now she's grown up, won Grammys and loads of other awards, and gotten married, so the look is more blown out and soft—gone is the pageantry. The color and styling are more natural, which really works for the huge stage she's on now."

Gone are the big printed floral dresses that worked for her back in 2005. With the help of her stylist, Trish Townsend, she has created some very beautiful, bright, or sleek and sophisticated red carpet looks. She doesn't wear anything that overwhelms her unless she is going onstage. Carrie hovers close to five-foot-three, so her stylist picks clothing that enhances rather than overwhelms her frame. Townsend says: "Carrie's style will evolve along with her music. She is the inspiration of the vision. I find style inspiration to correspond to the music she creates—that's why fashion suits her so well."

Grammy Awards, January 31, 2010

Victoria Beckham, Spice Girls, Billboard Music Awards, MGM Grand, Paradise, NV, December 1997

London, VH1 party, 1999

DEFINING AND DEVELOPING PERSONAL STYLE

Angelina Jolie, Katie Holmes, Victoria Beckham, Sienna Miller—they all have amazing personal style. All have experienced major fame, very serious relationships, and have maintained certain images while evolving with the times. These are women who have allowed their looks to develop along the way. They don't jump and throttle trends and layer themselves with the newest, the hottest, the most sensational, but they work with what they have and add and layer a few pieces here and there.

Angelina Jolie was in leather on the red carpet in her early years, then became highly sophisticated by wearing beautifully cut gowns and making her hair softer. Sarah Jessica Parker went from the lead role in *Annie* to a lovable geek to a California girl to Carrie Bradshaw in her Manolos and Vivienne Westwood. The Olsen twins literally grew up on the carpet. We watched them transform from little girls in matching sailor outfits to fashion forces to be reckoned with.

It's not only the clothing that evolves. Hair can make a big statement about where a person is in her life or career. After marrying Tom Cruise, Katie Holmes went from tousled to chic with her chop; Victoria Beckham lost the extensions and became more iconic with her pixie cut.

I've gathered here pictures and ideas to illustrate how our favorite ladies have very publicly made their transformations.

St. Tropez, June 2005

Costume Institute Ball, Metropolitan Museum of Art, New York, May 2006

VICTORIA BECKHAM

Victoria Beckham is a terrific example of a major transformation. Here, stylist Jill Swid, who has worked with Uma Thurman and Kristin Chenoweth, breaks down how Beckham went from bubblegum pop star to major designer force.

December 1997, Billboard Music Awards

"She juxtaposed punk with a soft touch—a feminine punk—which is just cool. She was in with the times. But what ruined it? A lot of people think it was her cheese-ball hair and makeup. There was no coolness to it."

January 1, 1999, VH1 Party

"This is when she became Hollywood, she became classy. Her body changed and she came into money. There's no one I know who wears a dress better than her, honestly. I've never seen a dress wear her. Her seamstress is brilliant. The way she looks, Victoria's just ready for the paparazzi. I don't mean, like, on a Sunday morning she would never wear flip-flops and not have makeup on. But there's an aura about her—I never really see that relaxed, calm feeling."

2005

"This look probably had a lot [to do with] David. Victoria Beckham looks rich. Everything about her just screams luxe and rich, like she's ready to go on her yacht with Barry Diller, and I love it. I love to see what she's wearing, and so do a lot of other people."

Marc Jacobs Fashion Show, New York, September 11, 2006

Launch of dVb denim and sunglasses at Saks
Fifth Avenue, New York, June 2007

**May 1, 2006, Costume Institute Gala's AngloMania
Exhibition at the Metropolitan Museum of Art**
"This is her wanting to be fun. If she's not sleek, then she
misses. It's always an amazing short little dress [by some-
one] who I don't know half the time. She has great taste."

**September 11, 2006, Marc Jacobs Fashion
Show during Olympus Fashion Week**
"This Marc Jacobs outfit is crème de la crème. I love it.
Victoria never tries to be cool. I think everyone tries to be
cool, to have an edge. But she never has it, and she doesn't
care to, obviously, and that's why she looks great all the
time. She doesn't try to be younger. She's a woman."

**June 14, 2007, dVb denim and sunglasses launch,
New York City**
"I love everything. It's fabulous, cheery, fun, sexy. I think she
actually looks a little Pamela Anderson or Jenny McCarthy.
Like she should be in that old Candies ad."

**August 7, 2009, *American Idol* auditions,
Denver, Colorado**
"I like that she can carry any color in the world. All these
colors look neutral on her. A popping magenta still looks
like a neutral when, for all of us, it would look silly. Even
though she's putting on this structured and amazing dress,
it's effortless. It doesn't seem overbearing on her at all. She's
not taking runway to reality. She's reality. It's amazing. In
America, she has the best taste of anyone, hands down. She
knows how to wear every designer. She doesn't save any
of her looks for the red carpet; she does it every day. She
should be First Lady. She screams fashion. She's sexy and
chic and rich."

In her own design at the *American Idol* Denver Auditions, August 2009

Sarah Jessica Parker, New York, April 1987

New York Ballet Spring Gala, New York, May 2004

SARAH JESSICA PARKER

I spoke with MaryAlice Stephenson, one of the world's most sought-after fashion and style experts. She's highly regarded as a knowledgeable commentator covering the latest trends in fashion, beauty, and lifestyle for many networks and shows, including CNN's *Anderson Cooper 360°*, MTV, VH1, ABC's *Good Morning America*, CBS's *Early Show*, *Extra*, E!, the Style Channel, and BBC.

Stephenson says: "Women love SJP because she is perfectly imperfect! We have all seen her fashion faux pas and they feel like our own. Who hasn't had a bad hair moment they would rather forget or seen a picture of themselves and thought, *'What the hell was I thinking!'* Women identify with her because they feel that if Sarah Jessica can look this good after looking that bad then why can't I! SJP is the fashion horse we all want to be. She's tried all the over-the-top clothes we wish we had the nerve to try ourselves. Her fashion icon status is admired because we all feel she has truly earned it."

"SJP is one of the hardest-working people I know," observes Stephenson, "and her successes in life comes from total dedication to doing things well and giving her all. I think for SJP, her style was not innate. She learned from her sisters, her friends, and all the great stylists she has worked

with. This shot (above) best illustrates the moment Sarah Jessica found her own style. She took her quirkiness, mixed in elegance, and created a star style that was instantly iconic and utterly SJP."

May 2004, New York Ballet Spring Gala

"Her fashion choices during this time all had common ingredients that gave everything she wore a wow factor. She had fun with dramatic clothes and understood that by wearing pieces with extreme volume, color, or pattern she could give the fashion-loving world what they craved: red carpet looks that had a look-at-me factor—serious fashion worn tongue-in-cheek! The clothes she wore on the red carpet proved to be the perfect combination to elevate her fashion status."

May 24, 2010, *Sex and the City 2* Premiere, New York

"The red carpet dresses Sarah Jessica wears now show more skin and are tighter, brighter, and feminine. They're also more minimal and have a graphic edge. Gone are all of the bells and whistles SJP used to be known for. Instead, a more sophisticated, elegant style has taken its place."

Sex and the City 2 premiere, New York, 2010

Nicole Richie, Miss Sixty and Energie L.A. store opening, West Hollywood, November 2003

TV Guide and Inside TV party, Hollywood, CA, September 2005   Carousel Ball, Beverly Hills, October 2008

NICOLE RICHIE

I asked Stacy London what she thought of early Nicole Richie style on the red carpet. Here's what she said:

"Nicole Richie's transformation has to be one of the most dramatic. At the beginning of her career, Nicole's style was outrageous, in-your-face, almost shocking: bright, even neon colors, two-tone hair, lots of skin, and high-top sneakers that did nothing to flatter the length of her legs.

Her fashion transformation seems to have coincided with her dramatic weight loss, but, truth be told, I don't think it was dependent on it. While she often wore revealing clothes when *very* thin, there is an elegance, an appropriateness to Nicole's choices. She dresses in a way that reflects her acknowledgment of red carpet glamour and her legacy and takes advantage of her frame. Instead of short, strapless tube dresses, she now wears full-length, choosing the sophistication of beading and more monochromatic colors to reflect her more serious attitude. While her style

was further transformed by becoming a serious jewelry designer and a mom, her look further evolved into something softer, less wild child, with flowier pieces, soft prints, and darker hair."

October 25, 2008, Carousel of Hope

"This red carpet event was a real change for Nicole," says Simone Harouche, who styles Richie as well as Christina Aguilera and Miley Cyrus. "After being mostly seen on the carpet in mod mini dresses, or long printed vintage gowns, Nicole wanted to shake things up. Again, not one to always play it safe, Nicole went with a gown that was completely opposite of what people expect from her: beaded, sophisticated, mature, and glamorous. This was also a couple months after Nicole had given birth to Harlow. She was feeling sexy and beautiful. She was proud of her curves and figure and wanted to show it off. She loved this look."

Nicole Richie for A Pea in the Pod, launch party, August 6, 2009

**August 6, 2009, Launch party of Nicole
Richie for A Pea in the Pod maternity line**

Harouche says, "Nicole was about seven months pregnant in this picture! Now, you tell me what other mom can rock a look like this [wearing her own line for a Pea in the Pod to boot!]. She feels comfortable in her skin, no matter what size she is. And I think that really shows here. She was proud of her body and not afraid to show it. I love her for that!"

January 16, 2010, Art of Elysium

"This look for me is classic Nicole. [Designer label] Etro's prints are so beautiful and the color choices are always spot on. When I saw this dress, I knew Nicole needed it. To me, this dress sums up Nicole's fashion sensibilities at the moment and also brings her style full circle from where it started. At her heart she is a bohemian, a free spirit. She loves bright prints, rich colors, and flowy dresses. She also loves to be comfortable in her clothes. This Etro dress is a slightly more sophisticated look but one that has its roots and inspiration in bohemian aesthetics and 1970s style," Harouche observes.

"At the end of the day, Nicole is a woman, just like all of us, with good days and bad. But she also knows how to choose pieces that she feels good in, no matter what. She knows what works for her and she looks effortless because she is not trying to follow a trend or be someone she is not. She gravitates toward easier, looser silhouettes. When you feel good in your clothes, people can tell. Women just give off a different air about themselves when they feel good. That's why I tend to go against trends for the sake of just being in style at the moment. You have to go with what works for your body, your personality, and what feels good. The confidence of feeling good in the clothes you are wearing makes people take notice." Haruche says.

London adds: "Richie's signature style is ever changing and evolving, but she has always maintained a deep sense of her own personality, and that's why it never looks like the clothes are wearing her. She has such a strong love of fashion. She is not afraid to step out of the box of conventional fashion and is always open to trying new things. She does not follow current trends or buy into the 'it bag' of the season. Her choices in clothing are timeless and can sustain all the changing trends.

"She goes for strong statement pieces, whether they be her love of the chiffon printed maxi gown or an amazing vintage clutch. Nicole knows how to mix and match subtle and strong pieces, which gives her looks an authentic voice."

The Art of Elysium Third Annual Black Tie Charity
Gala, Beverly Hills, January 2010

ABC TV Party, New York, May 1993

MARY-KATE AND ASHLEY OLSEN

Cher Coulter has styled Hollywood's elite, including red
carpet favorites Kate Bosworth, Michelle Williams, Orlando
Bloom, and Eric Bana. I asked her to look at the Olsen twins,
who have captivated us since their infancy, and share her
thoughts on what separates them from the pack.

Coulter says: "I think the fact they have been walking the
red carpet since an age when they were learning to walk is
why they are so individual and confident now. They don't
conform to safety on the carpet. They are always on trend
with their own sense of style.

"I think Mary-Kate's style is more bohemian, and
Ashley's is sleeker, but both are well thought out and executed perfectly. MK goes for it more with accessories and
lengths; she layers more and takes more risks. Ashley refines
things more but will take risks with a certain designer or
style of dress rather than the accessories; she is the more
classic of the two.

"Their style is iconic because they keep it evolving
and always remain one step ahead. Sometimes they may
end up on the 'who wore it worst' or 'what were they thinking?' pages, but ultimately they will always make it into
Vogue magazine.

"They understand the 'cycle of fashion,' which is what
I was taught in fashion design college: Everything moves
around and is in and out in a heartbeat. We may go from
obsessing over Chloe to Calvin in one six-month swoop.
Their understanding of fashion mixed with being brave
is what earns them icon status. Fashion is something that
involves risks—as long as you have proportions right and
wear looks with confidence, you can't go wrong."

MOMA Film Benefit, A Tribute to Tim Burton, New York, November 2009

Mary-Kate Olsen and Ashley Olsen pose in front of the winners boards at the Elle Style Awards 2010 held at The Grand Connaught Rooms in London, February 22, 2010

Katie Holmes, 11th Annual Nickelodeon Kids' Choice Awards, April 1998

Emmy Awards, Los Angeles, September 1998

First Daughter premiere, New York, September 2004

KATIE HOLMES

Janice Min was my editor in chief at *Us Weekly* and hired me over there. She's writing books now about sexy celebrity moms and is the editor of *The Hollywood Reporter*. Since she was there at the dawning of every TomKat move, I felt that she would be the perfect person to document the red carpet evolution and transformation of Mrs. Tom Cruise.

April 4, 1998, Nickelodeon Kids' Choice

"I remember this as the era when Prada was really getting big, and that whole minimalist look was big," recalls Min. "But something about that look works on New York City editors but not on celebrities so much. I bet she thought she looked grown up. And long sleeves to a premiere? That's only reserved for Dame Judy Dench. Everyone now, no matter what age, is about showing off her body. But when you are young and not sure of yourself, you usually err on the side of safety."

September 13, 1998, Emmy Awards

Min says, "Could she look more miserable? She's never been the kind of woman who looks like she wants to devour the camera but rather like someone who is not sure what she is doing there. I think she genuinely likes acting but maybe not the showman part of it. She looks like she's the best-dressed girl at her prom. This is the kind of outfit you'd wear when you are in your early twenties trying to look older. It's a common mistake for women who might not be born with the most innate style sense, which is just about everyone, to dress older rather than younger. That way you draw less attention to yourself."

September 22, 2004, *First Daughter* red carpet premiere party

"Now she's beginning to look like she's enjoying herself," Min comments. "The top is pretty racy for her. This is like 'after-hours Katie.' I like it. The hair is great too: easy. Not

FiFi Awards, New York, April 2005

Rome, April 2005

Mission Impossible III screening, Hollywood, May 2006

red carpet hair, but when you are in your mid-twenties you can get away with it. She seems to be much more confident of herself, and it shows. On its own that dress is nothing great, to be honest, but because she looks so confident the whole thing works."

April 7, 2005, FiFi Awards

"She's never really had a signature look, but clearly someone on her team decided she needed an Audrey Hepburn moment. Let's not forget this was right after she split with Chris Klein and before she was starting to see Tom Cruise. This might have been her last moment of independence. This is probably the official beginning of her ladylike phase, which she continues to have. She looks very comfortable," Min observes.

April 29, 2005, David di Donatello Awards

Min says, "It is clear from this picture that Katie is debuting 'grown-up Katie': the movie star boyfriend, the designer dress, and a look that is a bit more risqué than anyone is used to from her. She's usually not someone who draws attention to her chest, but this was one exception."

May 4, 2006, *Mission Impossible III* premiere two weeks and two days after Suri is born

Min exclaims, "Yikes! Too much hair, too much bow. But honestly, what are you supposed to look like two weeks after giving birth? She looks like she's in a complete new-mother daze. I think that sometimes we all put too much pressure on each other to get out right away and prove that motherhood hasn't changed us. But it does! There is probably no worse time to try to go out than in those first few months after you give birth, when nothing looks quite right on you still. So kudos to her for even trying."

Vanity Fair Oscar Party, February 2007

New York premiere of *Hairspray*, Ziegfeld Theater, July 2007

February 25, 2007, The *Vanity Fair* After-Oscar Party

"Perfection. This is a woman who's come into her style stride. She always seemed like she wished she were three inches shorter, but here she looks comfortable with her height, and everything about the look is elegant and pretty: the makeup, the hair jewels, the color of the dress. And instead of looking like she borrowed someone's dress, she makes this look hers all the way," observes Min.

July 16, 2007, *Hairspray* premiere

"What's interesting about this look," notes Min, "is it shows the power of the right dress. She actually looks younger here than she does in that picture taken nine years ago. Sometimes less is more, and while I wouldn't have minded a little bit of jewelry here, I like that she kept it simple. Also, this is the kind of look you can pull off when you feel good about your body. There is more skin showing here than dress, and she looks great. She even kept the hair and makeup clean and simple."

Welcome to L.A. Party for Victoria and David
Beckham, MOCA, Los Angeles, July 2007

23rd Annual Museum of the Moving Image Salutes Tom Cruise,
Cipriani 42nd St., New York, November 2007

**July 22, 2007, Welcome to L.A. Party
for Victoria and David Beckham**

"She was one of the hosts that evening, and she stepped out in a color she rarely wears. The thing is, when you wear red, you want to get noticed. Whereas Katie used to look like she wanted to recede into the background, here she looks confident with all eyes on her. The smile on her face says it all. If you are going to wear this color, mean it, and she does. This is the kind of confidence you can't fake. So you have to get yourself in a happy place on your own—no outfit will help you with that," says Min.

**November 6, 2007, 23rd Annual Museum
of the Moving Image Salutes Tom Cruise,
at Cipriani 42nd street, New York**

"Incredible: the slick straight bob, the dark velvet, the cat-who-ate-the-canary smile. She looks amazing, and she knows it. One of the things I like about Katie's style is that she's not a cleavage-shower. Her sexiness comes from selling sophistication, not sex. There aren't a lot of actresses who can pull that off; most are too insecure, trying to prove to the world that they have boobies or great thighs. Katie is too classy a dresser to do that," says Min.

Sienna Miller, *Layer Cake* premiere, London, September 23, 2004

Casanova premiere, Los Angeles, November 2005

SIENNA MILLER

Aside from being one of the best looking men in fashion, Adam Glassman has been the creative director of *O, the Oprah Magazine* since 2000, styling Ms. Winfrey for the cover each month. I asked him to discuss Sienna Miller's style over the years.

September 2004, *Layer Cake* premiere

"In 2004, everyone really started to take notice of Sienna—not only of her acting but also her amazing fashion sense. She has an English artist-boho chic sensibility, like Kate Moss. You can tell that she feels comfortable in her skin, and her style reflects her personality: young, fresh, fun, fearless, and a little bit rebellious. She understands how to mix high-end designer clothing with thrift store and vintage pieces, which is key to her look. The dress over the jeans, belted, with the embellished motorcycle boots creates a cool downtown hipster look. This look started the whole idea of layering a short dress over pants."

November 2005, *Casanova* premiere

"When Sienna cut her hair into a short pixie look it was a modern riff on Edie Sedgwick, whom she played in *Factory Girl*. She set off a trend for short short hair. She also brought back the shoulder-duster earring trend, here wearing long, gold DVF for H. Stern earrings."

September 2005, London

"She has an innate sense about what works on her body and she makes fashion look fun. Her look is completely understandable: It is casual ease, like she just threw it on

Outside the Wyndham Theatre, London, September 9, 2005

Factory Girl premiere, London, March 2007

BET Studios visit, New York Image, August 3, 2009

Screening of *G.I. Joe: The Rise of Cobra,* Los Angeles, August 6, 2009

without much thought, and yet it all looks perfect. And she definitely has her favorite things, which she wears over and over again. I remember a period of about a year when you never saw her without her black Balenciaga motorcycle purse, then one summer it was all about the porkpie hat! That boho chic dress in a bold colored print, Sienna paired it with a suede slouchy boot, a look we had really not seen since the late '70s. The knit cap adds to her offbeat, effortless chic."

March 2007, *Factory Girl* premiere

"Wearing a white dress with opaque black tights on the red carpet was really directional, and it ignited the comeback of black hose."

August 2009

"The Isabel Marant studded booties are very '80s, and by pairing them with a mini dress, Sienna gave them a new look that so many young women embraced and are still wearing today."

August 2009, *G.I. Joe* screening

"Sienna grew out her hair and she wore it in a wonderful Veronica Lake/Old Hollywood style with deep lipstick, paired with an ethereal Yves Saint Laurent dress."

November 2009

"Sienna Miller is a real fashion person: always glamorous, whether she is walking her dog or walking the red carpet. She's in another trendsetting look with this 'call of the

Sienna Miller walking her dog in New York, November 2009

Costume Institute Ball, May 3, 2010

wild' short, fluffy jacket thrown over layered T-shirts. Paired with leggings, it really shows how Sienna plays with proportion, always choosing looks that work for her body."

May 2010, Costume Institute Ball

Glassman says: "At the Met Ball in 2010 in Emilio Pucci, Sienna really came into her own: she is comfortable in her own skin. The first thing we noticed, of course, is Sienna's beauty, the sexy goddess that she is, arm in arm with her on-again beau, Jude Law. The outfit was really secondary, as it should be for someone with true personal style, but the look was classic Sienna: effortlessly rumpled chic and a fabulous hairstyle that looked like she just pinned a few pieces back herself, no fuss. She looked like Sienna, not an overly made-up version of herself. It was a refreshing take on red carpet chic, and she blew us away with her unique brand of laid-back glamour."

"Like so many movie-star style icons, Sienna is always under the microscope, with every outfit analyzed and critiqued. Maintaining your standing on the best-dressed lists is not easy to do, and through the years she's made a few missteps, but she really has branded herself with her quirky bohemian look. And she is influential: When she wore long scarves, long necklaces, and tunics, everyone copied her; when she cut her hair, some of the world's most glamorous women followed—or at least considered it! I think women everywhere can learn from Sienna: Dress in a way that feels natural, not 'put on,' like a costume. Wear things you love, find your signature look, and experiment!"

Playing God premiere, 1997

2000 Academy Awards, winner Best Supporting Actress,
Girl, Interrupted, Los Angeles, March 2000

ANGELINA JOLIE

Susan Swimmer is the fashion features editor of *More* magazine and the author of *Michelle Obama: First Lady of Fashion and Style*. Here she walks us through Angelina Jolie's style evolution.

"We've watched Angelina the Wild Child transform into Angelina the Earth Mother, her look evolving as the stages in her life unfold," remarks Swimmer. "The woman who once stood on the red carpet tongue-kissing Billy Bob Thornton—with a vial of his blood dangling from her neck— is now traveling the globe fighting for human rights with a baby on each hip. Her twentysomething look was dominated by a black leather uniform—it made her appear hard and unapproachable, a persona she seemed to want to cultivate. But as her life has taken her to activism and motherhood, she's dressing for a different part. What's stayed the same? Simple silhouettes, body-revealing styles, strong shoulders. What's changed? That same style has been utterly transformed into something more mature, more glamorous, and more feminine simply by changing the fabrics and colors. The harshness of leather has been replaced by soft chiffons; the all-black color scheme has been replaced with buff, taupe, gray, yellow, and white. She's given a rethink to the no-jewelry look—today she often chooses face-framing statement earrings—and hair is kept soft."

2004 Academy Awards, Los Angeles, February 2004

Mr. and Mrs. Smith premiere, Los Angeles, 2005

October 1997, *Playing God* red carpet premiere

"In a long black leather trench coat with very pale skin, it's clear she wants to play the bad girl and distinguish herself from the rest of the Hollywood good girls of the time," says Swimmer.

March 2000, Academy Awards

"Here, as the ultimate rebel, she wore the anti-Oscar look [in a black Versace gown]. She's trying not to make a statement but in turn makes a huge statement," notes Swimmer.

February 2004, Academy Awards

"Suddenly glamorous," remarks Swimmer, "this is Jolie starting to position herself as a screen siren—and a Hollywood power player. It's one of her first forays into a softer silhouette—and color! This is also when she moved to shiny natural brown hair with soft curls."

June 2005, *Mr. and Mrs. Smith* premiere

Swimmer remarks, "Never sexier, Jolie manages to find the style intersection between power bitch and screen siren. Who knew skin-tight black leather could look so . . . stately? This is a quintessential Jolie look."

The Good Shepherd premiere, New York, December 2006

Ocean's Thirteen premiere, Cannes Film Festival, May 2007

December 2006, *Good Shepherd* premiere

"Our bisexual knife wielder is all grown up! Jolie's style evolves again. She keeps to her favorite color palette of black-gray-taupe, but the look is more feminine and understated," says Swimmer.

May 2007, *Ocean's Thirteen* premiere, Cannes

"Here she wears sunny yellow in sunny Cannes," observes Swimmer. "As she has grown older she has lightened up her look with color and fabrics. The dress, a modern take on a Grecian goddess, done in a color that has come to symbolize peace the world over, proves that Jolie is not only a shrewd power player—the ultimate Hollywood alpha female—but also a woman at the apex of her own style story. Wearing that dress at this time really says it all—Jolie has become the woman she is meant to be."

HOW TO DEVELOP YOUR OWN PERSONAL STYLE

BY ADAM GLASSMAN

YOU CAN WEAR ANYTHING as long as you are confident—commit to your choices and wear them with pride. Experiment and have fun. Stay open to new trends because, until you try them, you really have no idea how they can work (or not!) on your body.

You can get inspiration and ideas from almost anywhere. Make a point of people-watching. For me, the streets of NYC, L.A., Paris, and London are endlessly inspiring. Start collecting images from magazines and catalogs, go through books, and search the Internet for famous style icons. Soon you'll have a folder full of inspirational looks and people—then you can compare and contrast everything so you can figure out what your personal style is.

Do you love Audrey Hepburn in *Sabrina* and think Keira Knightley looks amazing walking arm-and-arm with her boyfriend? Maybe your style is *gamine*. Do you admire Grace Kelly's cool elegance and think that Gwyneth Paltrow looked her best in *The Talented Mr. Ripley*? Then you're probably *a classic sophisticate*. If you love Stevie Nicks's gypsy style or Talitha Getty's caftans, I'd say you're all about a *'70s California* vibe.

Next, shop your closet. Take inventory: what do you have, and what do you need to fill in the gaps? Be brutal with yourself or, better yet, ask a friend for help—someone you trust who will be honest about how things look on you.

See if you can re-create some of the looks you admire with your own clothes; this will also make it easier to figure out what you need to complete your look. Want to be boho-chic like Sienna Miller? You need some long scarves. On-trend like Beyoncé? You need a statement shoe. Hipster-hippie like Drew Barrymore? If you can't find those Wayfarers from high school, you'd better add them to your wish list.

Playing with your own existing clothes in new ways is also economical. Find a good tailor to alter and modify pieces that you own: A black sheath dress at the back of your closet can be shortened into a mini with a flirty slit. And what is sexier than an old sweatshirt cut up to create an '80s rocker look (hello, Pat Benatar)?

When you finally start shopping, start with accessories first: jewelry, shoes, scarves, bags, hats. They instantly update and change an outfit. And until you've really honed your style, don't spend a lot of money on trendy items; trends come and go in a flash these days, so I always recommend shopping at stores like H&M, Topshop, and Zara for fun pieces that won't break the bank. Once you feel truly comfortable in your look, start making investments in pieces that will last—and that you will love—forever.

CHAPTER SIX

The 4-1-1 on Avoiding a 9-1-1

Things go wrong. The dress separated at the seams when your client got out of the car. The bodice of the strapless dress squeezed your client's flesh out over the top. Coca-Cola spilled onto the one-of-a-kind haute couture Valentino dress on loan to you from a designer who's already sold it to a princess in Dubai. Your trunks went to Houston when they were supposed to arrive in L.A. These things happen. Instead of collapsing and dying (and sometimes you will believe death is the only solution), you'll have to figure out a way to, and I quote the iconic reality-television star Tim Gunn, "Make it work."

In this chapter you'll find all sorts of tips on how to *make it work* and how to survive a near catastrophe. You'll learn stain-removal secrets, shapewear must-haves, how to find a tailor, and more.

MISSED CONNECTIONS; OR, THE HAZARDS OF TRAVELING WITH TRUNKS

There is nothing worse than hearing the words "The package is stuck in customs," or "It didn't make the pickup," or "It's marked for Monday delivery." Same with looking for a gown on a rack and not finding it there—or anywhere. Sending a garment from point A to point B has its risks, for sure, but you don't have to be part of the casualty. Read on to learn from three different scenarios.

"THE TRUNKS ARE IN HOUSTON . . ."

Recently, on my way to L.A. for an *Us Weekly* shoot, I received a call about forty-five minutes before my flight departed, telling me that trunks filled with clothing for two celebrity shoots had not been delivered to my hotel as expected but ended up in Houston. I laughed. Kind of. Years ago, I would have cried and screamed, but now I know it's best to be calm in a crisis. Modern technology is a wonderful thing. Years ago, stylists didn't have cell phones, e-mail, or other resources at their fingertips. Since I knew the flight was five hours long, I hustled with my team to jump-start a new plan of action. We called UPS and told them to reroute the trunk to L.A. for next-day early-morning delivery to my hotel. We also e-mailed and phoned our resources in L.A. to borrow the same or similar pieces as the ones we had put together. Luckily, everything was sorted out before the plane was airborne. I was also lucky the shoot wasn't in a remote location where there's no hub or delivery center.

Your best defense in a scenario like this is to have a backup plan or get one real quick. Do this calmly and quickly. Make phone calls, send e-mails, and even put others on your team to work for you—especially if you're tied up, like on a plane. Call studio services at department stores like Saks Fifth Avenue, Barneys, or Bloomingdales, or have your team call boutiques that are near your hotel when you land, to try to borrow clothing; call a magazine editor who may have a collection nearby; phone a seamstress or someone who could literally whip up a dress in a heartbeat. Don't waste time and energy getting mad, screaming, or crying. That does no one any good.

Also make very stern calls to the carrier. Tell the company how imperative it is that the mixup be fixed and the package delivered. If the garment went to another part of the country, demand that it be found, put on another plane, and sent immediately to the correct address. In my more than twenty years' experience, stuff like this happens more often than not. Since this practice has almost become the norm, I

MACGYVER MOMENTS

THE MOST FAMOUS FASHION MACGYVER MOMENT belongs to Sharon Stone. For the 1996 Oscars, legend has it that she had several gowns arrive from Armani, Vera Wang, and everyone else from NYC to Rome, yet nothing worked. Stone said, "I thought, 'A Gap T-shirt to the Oscars? Hey, I'm nominated [for *Casino*] and presenting two Oscars, so why not have some attitude?" She ended up pairing that Gap turtleneck with a Valentino ready-to-wear skirt and a season-old Armani dress worn as a coat. Voilà! Wanda McDaniel, executive VP of Global Communications for Giorgio Armani, told me Sharon Stone called her and exclaimed, "You will never guess what I'm wearing to the Oscars!"

Another red carpet quick-fix maneuver was born when Cameron Diaz, Drew Barrymore, and Lucy Liu were on the carpet for *Charlie's Angels*. Diaz was walking across the street when her Christian Louboutin cork stiletto heel broke off. It was a potential fashion emergency with a towering Diaz about to tip onto the pavement. So she did what supermodels do when they fall on the runway—she took off the heels and walked to the premiere barefoot.

Sharon Stone, 68th Academy Awards, March 1996

Lucy Liu, Cameron Diaz, and Drew Barrymore, *Charlie's Angels: Full Throttle* premiere, Los Angeles, June 2003

always travel with my clothing now. The biggest obstacles then are that the airlines not only charge you for baggage overweight (each carrier is different, so call ahead if you know you're traveling with heavy suitcases), but they will allow only a specific length onboard. So if you travel with the black trunks, or "coffins," as they're affectionately called, be aware that you may be charged a fee for oversize luggage. If possible, go with crushable hockey or rolling bags. Call ahead and see what you're allowed to fly with, and always travel with an extra, foldable duffel bag.

MISSING IN ACTION

Penny Lovell, who works with Ginnifer Goodwin and Rose Byrne, told me: "Luckily—and fingers crossed—I haven't had too many loss or damage experiences. But once, during Oscar season, a dress must have fallen off our rack [en route] to a fitting. We searched for days. Fortunately the designer was amazingly understanding. Losing something is always a risk and one of our biggest fears. My assistant is very diligent about taking care of samples. Without our good relationships with designers, we have nothing, so it's important to be very respectful of their clothes. Pieces fail to arrive for shoots on time every now and then, but we allow for that by making sure we have enough pulled locally and in our possession. For events, we don't take any risks—once a dress has been chosen it stays with us until the event. We also have a backup dress in case something very unexpected happens." (See also Lovell's interview, page 26, for more stories you can learn from.)

It is horrifying to accept that a piece of clothing has disappeared on your watch. As Lovell said, it's extremely important to maintain great relationships with the designers and showrooms who regularly lend to you. And how to prevent an unhappy customer who was counting on that look? Always have a backup garment and a solid plan.

DELIVERY DUD

Robert Verdi told me how he avoided a potentially disastrous moment for his client, Eva Longoria, one of the stars of *Desperate Housewives:* "I was waiting for a package to arrive on a Saturday morning—the awards were on a Sunday—but it was mistakenly sent for Monday delivery. Oh, my God. In that moment, that's your reality. It's not the reality people imagine to be a stylist's life: drinking champagne at a party with celebrities and sitting in the front row of a fashion show. The reality is rushing to FedEx to figure out how to get the package rerouted, then finding a tailor in New Orleans who can actually alter a haute couture dress that just arrived from Paris, cleared customs, and is in a van on its way to the hotel. Everything has to be timed properly, otherwise the celebrity is going to be in a sweatsuit on the red carpet. I had to find a driver who was available and willing to drive three hours. I had to find a seamstress who could actually tailor well without cutting any fabric. Luckily everything worked out. But after a situation like this, you do feel like you earned a few new gray hairs." Be sure to read Verdi's interview on page 72.

Again, having a calm mind will allow you to think fast on your feet. Finding people to do last-minute work can be extremely unnerving, but if you know what's entailed, and thoroughly go over the details with them, who knows, you might have earned yourself a few new keeper contacts.

ON SPOT

What happens when a celebrity lets a wee bit of soda stain a couture gown worth $125,000? This happened to me when I was working on a cover for the annual *Us Weekly* style issue. Hilary Duff was wearing a glorious gown lent to us for a cover with Lauren Conrad and Taylor Swift. Duff was thirsty. She grabbed a Coke and sipped and . . . dribble dribble dribble out of the straw and onto the dress went the soda. I almost died. I couldn't run the dress off the set to have it cleaned, because we needed to rush to get the shot. I moved quickly, retrieved my stain-remover kit, and washed off the spot before it set. Thank God I had my kit on hand.

For more than half a century, Madame Paulette Cleaners in New York has been the leader and pioneer in couture, bridal, and interior cleaning and restoration. John Mahdessian, who owns and operates the family-run business, says that time is the most important factor in stain removal—it's imperative to treat the spot immediately.

First, don't panic. Second, use a spoon to remove any excess staining matter that's left on the garment. Third, reach for your Madame Paulette Professional Stain Kit, which should be stashed in your prop kit or evening bag. I recommend that every stylist have one. But if you don't have the kit, no worries. You can easily put together your own by following Mahdessian's advice for different types of stains. Before you begin to remove any stain, always test the solution on a hidden seam to make sure that the fabric can handle the removal.

BLOOD OR SWEAT STAINS

Unsightly blood and sweat stains don't have to be permanent—if you act fast. Follow these directions for removing them and your garment will be as good as new.

You'll need:
1 clean white towel
2 Q-tips or small, clean rags
Ice-cold water
Ammonia
Peroxide
Color-safe detergent, like Ivory Snow Liquid (1 oz.)
Small container (cup, bowl, etc.)

① Place a clean white towel behind the stain.

② Grab a Q-tip or small rag, depending on the size of the spot, and use *ice-cold* water to rewet the stain until the garment is soaked through. *Never* use hot or warm water on blood or sweat stains. Some of the stain should transfer onto the towel.

③ Mix together 4 parts water, 1 part ammonia, 1 part peroxide, and 1 part detergent in a small container.

④ Lightly dip a dry Q-tip or rag into the solution, then gently tap the stain, which should push through to the towel underneath. Rotate the absorbent cloth as the stain comes out.

COFFEE OR WINE STAINS

These are the most common stains, but luckily there's a solution.

You'll need:
Cold water
White absorbent cloth
2 small containers (cup, bowl, etc.)
Color-safe detergent, like Ivory Snow Liquid
2 Q-tips or small, clean rags
Color-safe bleach, like Clorox 2

① Flush the stain with cold water.

② Place a white absorbent cloth under the garment.

③ In a small container, mix together 3 parts water and 1 part detergent.

④ Use a Q-tip or small, clean rag to dab at the stain with the above mixture.

⑤ If the residue doesn't come out, mix 1 part water and 1 part color-safe bleach in a small container. Apply with a Q-tip or clean rag until the stain is gone.

OIL STAINS

Oily residues can result from pizza, hair gel, sauces, and greasy foods. But these smears don't have to stay on your clothes.

You'll need:
Clean white absorbent cloth
Small container (cup, bowl, etc.)
Clear dishwashing liquid
White vinegar
Q-tip or clean rag

① Place a clean white absorbent cloth under the stain.

② In a small container, mix 2 parts dishwashing liquid and 1 part white vinegar.

③ With a Q-tip or clean rag, dab the stain lightly with the solution to break it down. The stain should pass onto the towel underneath.

④ Flush the spot with lukewarm water.

INK OR MARKER STAINS

Depending on the clothing's fabric and type of ink (oil, water, or glue based), ink stains can be very difficult to remove at home. It is best to use the professional Madame Paulette Stain Kit or bring the garment to a professional cleaner.

The most common ink stains come from ballpoint pens, which are oil based. Nail polish remover is known to work on some fabrics but not all. *Do not* use any type of nail polish remover on synthetic fabrics such as rayon, acetate, or polyester. If your fabric is synthetic, and the stain is from an oil-based ink, try the following solution.

You'll need:
Clean white absorbent cloth
Small container (cup, bowl, etc.)
Water
Ammonia
Peroxide
Color-safe detergent, like Ivory Snow Liquid
Q-tip or clean rag

(1)   Place a clean white absorbent cloth under the stain.

(2)   In a small container, mix 5 parts water, 1 part ammonia, 1 part peroxide, and 1 part color-safe detergent.

(3)   Use the Q-tip or rag to lightly tap the stain with the solution. This should push the spot through to the cloth underneath. Rotate the absorbent cloth as the stain comes out.

Marilyn Monroe shapewear

SUCKING IT IN: STYLISTS' MAGICAL SECRETS

The quickest fix for getting a lean look for your client in that dress (without resorting to surgery) can be found in compression garments and body tapes made to lift, suck in, separate, contour, and shape the jiggles. These body shapers smooth all over and won't create rollovers or muffin tops. With all the skimpy, sheer, and revealing gowns on the red carpet these days, it's more important than ever to conceal bumps, ripples, bloating—whatever the body throws at you. Because God forbid anyone shows the slightest bit of flab—to do so is to invite all sorts of gossip. Women want seamless control. And though some male celebrity stylists pooh-pooh the idea of men's Spanx on their clients, they're in hot demand and available now.

TYPES OF SHAPEWEAR

There's an art to figuring out what body shaper to buy and for which area. Actresses now often arrive to fittings with their favorite slimmers. It's helpful to ask ahead of time so they don't forget to bring it along, or ask what kind they prefer so that you can be prepared with a selection you've purchased for them. I have never seen a stylist arrive without drawers or bags overflowing with these goods.

Waist controllers: Spanx Slim Cognito Seamless Mid-Thigh Bodysuit has a "soft" waistband that shapes the midriff and hips, and for a seamless look it also lifts up the rear. Stretchy and smooth across the body, it also has a few removable straps to attach to a bra. The leg band also eliminates bulging at the thigh. Rihanna's stylists Rob Zangardi and Mariel Haenn swear that Wacoal's Get in Shape Hi-Waist Shape Brief, a moderate-control shaper, is their styling secret weapon.

Midthigh shapers: If you're working with pencil-skirted suits, these are perfect for slimming the thighs while also holding in the tummy and butt. These undergarments pull everything in and eliminate visible panty lines. Assets Sensational Shaper provides tummy control and reduces bulges.

Beyoncé, *Good Morning America*, New York, September 2006

Q & A WITH SARA BLAKELY

The creator of Spanx, Sara Blakely, offers some hilarious, great insight to how her revolutionary brand came about and why she's so in demand.

YOUR BRAND IS AS WELL KNOWN AS Q-TIPS NOW. HOW DID YOU COME UP WITH SPANX?

It came from a personal need. I couldn't figure out what to wear under a pair of white pants that I'd spent my hard-earned money on. Every time I put on anything underneath, you could see it, and I had just a little bit of cellulite on the back of my thighs that made me not like the way it looked.

I was twenty-seven years old and went to look for body shapers for the first time in my life. I was a size 2. All the shapers I found were thick and uncomfortable and actually made me look heavier because of the material used. So I cut the feet out of my pantyhose one day and threw them on under my white pants—the look was flawless. I had no cellulite or panty line. The only problem was that the pantyhose rolled up my legs all night. So when I got home from the party that night, I thought, "If I can figure out a way to comfortably keep this just below the knee, this will be a home run for so many women who've got that one item hanging in their closet that they can't wear." That's what birthed Spanx.

HOW DID YOU COME UP WITH THE NAME SPANX?

I'd been brainstorming the name for a long time. I knew that Kodak and Coca-Cola are two of the most recognized names in the world, so I started playing with them in my mind, saying, "What do they have in common?" They both have a strong K sound. I did some research on the K sound, and I discovered that it's a weird trade secret among comedians that the K sound will make an audience laugh. After a year and a half of bad names I decided, "Whatever my name is going to be, I want it to have a strong K sound." Almost instantaneously, the word *spanks* came to me while I was sitting in traffic. At the last minute, I changed the *ks* to an *x*, and that's really how it happened.

One of the runner-ups was Open Toed Delilahs. I don't think I'd be talking to you right now if the name were Open Toed Delilahs.

Perhaps because the name is so fun, celebrities started popping it out of their mouths on the red carpet, which never happened before with an undergarment, making Spanx a household name. I think a lot of it had to do with the personality behind the brand and the fact that it really worked. Many women were jaded because they invested in products that promised the moon but ended up pinching their stomachs or rolling up and down. Spanx truly works for a lot of people, making them look and feel better in their clothes.

WHO WEARS SPANX?

A lot of my clients are size 0 and 2. Most of Hollywood wears Spanx, and they're all very thin and very fit. Spanx has many purposes, depending on the woman. For some women, it brings you down an entire size. Maybe you're a size 12 and you can wear your size 10 dress or pants in a certain Spanx. For other women, it's just about the panty line. They love clothing, and a lot of couture is very sheer, so it creates a barrier for them underneath clothes.

WHEN WAS THE FIRST TIME YOU HEARD A CELEBRITY MENTION SPANX ON THE RED CARPET?

A reporter said to Gwyneth Paltrow, "You look great," and she responded, "I'm wearing Spanx." When she was interviewed for *USA Today*, she said, "I wear Spanx. That's why I even look decent after having children. All the Hollywood girls do it, and a lot of us wear two pairs for award shows."

WHY DO YOU THINK CELEBRITIES AND STYLISTS ARE WILD ABOUT YOUR BRAND?

Because it works. I don't think they'd be talking about something and sharing that information wholeheartedly unless it was really working. The magic of Spanx is in the fit. A lot of other shapers just try to make it as tight as they can from top to bottom, and we realized you can't do that. If you squeeze everywhere, you're either going to get a bulge at the top or a bulge on the thigh, or [the slimmer] is just uncomfortable and doesn't move with your body. So we studied the areas where women need support, and we put the most compression there. We also relaxed certain parts of the garment so it all worked together without creating large lumps or bulges.

We spent endless days and months on fit, and that's what you really feel in the product. I invested much more in the test fitting than anybody had done for a long time. The hosiery and shapewear industry had become such a price-driven commodity that mills were just trying to make [products] as cheaply and quickly and efficiently as they could. Over time, it started backfiring on them because women stopped wearing pantyhose altogether, because they were so uncomfortable.

WHICH SPANX PIECE DO STYLISTS USE MOST OFTEN?

Anything high waisted. On the red carpet, the Slim Cognito Suit is truly body transforming. It's an investment piece that can last many, many years. There are a lot of celebrities who wear the Higher Power, which comes in the hosiery package. It's less expensive and a little bit more like underwear.

Globes season and the Oscars are crazy busy—we get calls all day long from everybody's stylists. Off the top of my head, we work with Rachel Zoe and Nicole Chavez. Celebs like Taraji Henson mentioned wearing Spanx. Tina Fey is always flashing hers, and so is Molly Shannon. And there's the actor from *The Office*, Rainn Wilson. It's hilarious. Every time he's interviewed on the red carpet, he says, "Well you know, it's really my Spanx I'd like to mention."

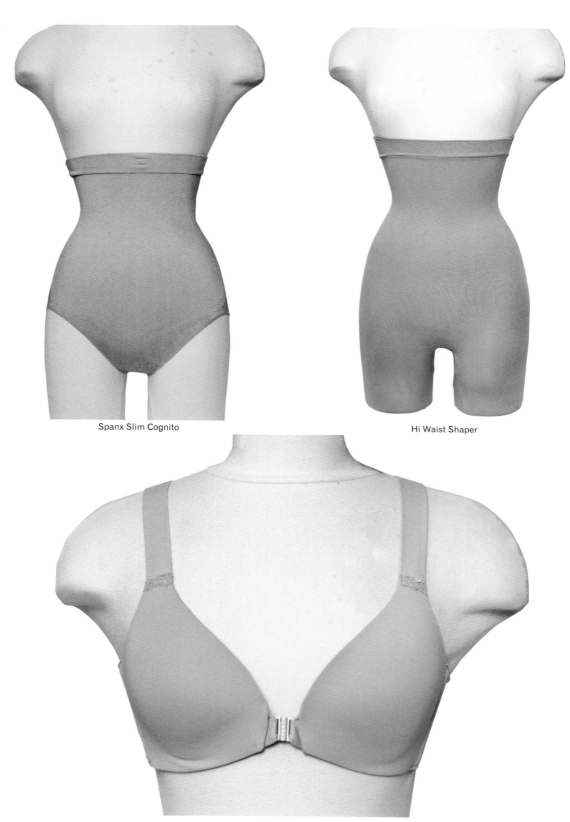

Spanx Slim Cognito

Hi Waist Shaper

Spanx Bra

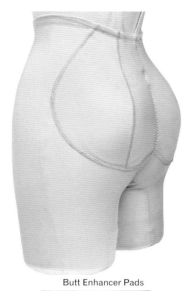

Butt Enhancer Pads

Strapless Plunge Backless Push Up Bra

Breast Enhancers

Butt Enhancer Pads

Takeouts Breast Enhancers

Back slimmers: Sassybax's Torso Trim has a built-in bra to smooth back fat and eliminate "bra bulge" under thin tops by compression. It also slims the waist. Maidenform's Ultimate Instant Slimmer Torsette, "with 360-degree shaping," promises to smooth back rolls. Or try Spanx's Bra-llelujah! Underwire Contour Front-Closure Bra. It's soft with control and gives no visible lines. Perfect for a smooth, sexy back.

Bottom enhancer: When you actually need to add some junk in the trunk for someone who may have a very flat rear, look no further than the Dr. Rey Shapewear Bottom Enhancer. This garment enhances the rear with removable pads and shapes, flatters thighs, and avoids ride up with a silicone gripper.

Backless bras: For low-back and no-back styles, Sassybax offers a seamless underwire bra that won't cling to clothing. With an adhesive inside top and bottom, it really sticks and holds. It's good for up to fifty wearings. Le Mystère is a great brand for bras that work with backless or halter cuts. Look for a strapless bra that wraps around the natural waist to sit low on the back. If your client is an A or B cup and she needs a bra for keyhole necklines, spaghetti straps, or off-the-shoulder or one-shoulder dresses or tops, try a polyester bra or a silicone bra with cups that adhere directly to the skin. For C cups and above, chose a thin polyurethane adhesive bra like those from Nubra or Fashion Forms.

Dr. Rey Shapewear Slip/Bra

Eva Mendes, Costume Institute Ball, New York, May 2009

Plunge controllers: Looking for a foundation that's sexy, slims and shapes, yet offers coverage for a plunging dress or top? The Dr. Rey Shapewear Deep Plunge slip is perfect. It comes in nude and black and offers flawless, flattering shaping. For bras that dip low, Dr. Rey Shapewear is an excellent resource, as is the tried-and-true Frederick's of Hollywood. Both have several features that help mold and give extra cleavage.

Breast enhancers: There are very few celebrity women on the carpet without some sort of padding, lifting, or smoothing out in the breast department. Every stylist keeps fake soft, round boobs on hand, and nowadays almost every actress arrives with her own set as well. Phillip Bloch says that "cutlets are a must" for boosting a dress that falls flat. As with everything, try them with the look beforehand. Make sure they are placed where they need to sit and are not upside down or punctured. Check out silicone bra inserts that go from light padding up to a two-cup increase. NuBra comes in mini, demi, small, large, and extra-large with self-adhesives. Takeouts from Commando come in clear and feel very natural. Top Hats are an important nipple concealer from Commando that are perfect for jersey and silk gowns.

Allure's prop kit is filled with cutlets, bras, and thongs in every shade of nude.

For men: Expert Lori Kaplan from Bra Tenders, a famous undergarments resource that has outfitted celebrities on Broadway and on the silver screen, tells me that "the man-siere is very popular now because men feel self-conscious about how they look in their clothing, especially if they're onstage or on screen. They want to look better." Male shapewear includes "mirdles," or man girdles, also known as support boxers. Go Softwear's Waist Eliminator brief has a waistband that extends up the midsection, pulling in love handles. The Form collection from 2(x)ist offers high-waist briefs that slim the waist. In the same collection, the Con-tour Pouch brief is designed to improve posture and smooth the waist, creating a sleeker silhouette. Slimming T-shirts or torso shapers are designed to be worn under slim-cut shirts. Spanx also has a line designed for men.

SHAPEWEAR BUYING TIPS

Here are a few nuggets of advice when shopping for slim-mers and enhancers for your client:

- Stay true to the size of your celebrity—going up a size doesn't work, won't get the job done, and will add more bulk or be a worse fit than before.
- Audition shapewear under the dresses and gowns they're intended for—do not leave this until the last minute. You need to see if it shapes, contours, smoothes, and other-wise does its job beforehand.
- Follow the garments's seams (if any), making sure that the shapewear is situated properly on your client.

Q & A WITH LORI KAPLAN

Lori Kaplan at Bra Tenders knows all about the all-important underpinnings that can take an actress or actor's physique down a size or two. She knows about bras, body slimmers, boy shorts, and the new contraption: a mirdle for the guys!

IF YOUR CLIENT IS WEARING SOMETHING THAT IS SHEER, WHAT WOULD BE THE PERFECT LINER OR SLIP TO GO UNDERNEATH TO MAKE SURE THAT YOUR CELEBRITY HAS PROPER COVERAGE?

I think that probably starts with the fitting. If it feels too sheer or too clingy, then it probably is, and nothing will make it look good. I look at all these actresses who are wearing strapless dresses that show spillage under their armpits because the dresses are just not fitted properly or it's just not the right shape or size. If you want to be styled, then get somebody who knows about making clothes.

And yes, there are undergarments that you can wear to help. One of our most popular products is a Spanx garment that comes all the way up under the bust. The Slim Cognito can be worn with or without a bra, and you can get it in a length that comes either just below the knee or just above the knee. It smoothes everything so nothing's bumpy or lumpy. But if your clothes are not properly fitted in the first place, it doesn't matter what undergarments you're wearing, it's not going to make a difference.

ARE THERE SPECIFIC SLIPS OR SLIMMERS THAT CAN TAKE A PERSON DOWN A FULL SIZE?

Yes, we make a couple of garments that were originally designed to be worn after surgery. After you have liposuction or a tummy tuck, you want to be as compressed as possible. These are very rigid garments that can take your waist down a couple of inches, but there's a little bit of bulk to them.

ARE MEN LOOKING FOR SHAPEWEAR?

There's been a recent trend of men's shapewear, for men who have a little paunch and want to look slimmer in their shirts without a bulge over their pants waist. Twenty years ago, almost all of men's underwear was bought for them by wives or girlfriends. Men are definitely taking more of an interest in their appearance and shopping for their own underwear, including slimming garments. The company 2(x)ist has a product that is like a high-waisted brief for men.

IS IT SEAMLESS?

It is not seamless. We get a lot of requests for seamless for men. But it's really hard to define the body in fabrics that don't have seams. It's like a woman's bra—everyone wants a seamless molded-cut bra, but the best shape for a woman's bust is a bra with three seams. The other problem with women and bras is that most women are wearing back sizes too big and cup sizes too small. When you buy a bra that's too big in the back, it rides up between your shoulder blades and then your boobs fall on your belly. It really bugs me when I see women with fat hanging out of their armpits in strapless dresses. There are alternatives, [such as] halters.

WHAT WOULD BE ESSENTIAL THINGS TO INCLUDE IN A STYLIST'S PROP KIT?

The most important thing is two-sided tape. And then a pair of breast pads or cutlets in the most universal size. You should also include a thong or a brief and some kind of shaper garment, like a Spanx or a body wrap. Then a laser-cut slip for lining sheer garments, and breast petals to cover the nipples. We carry a product called Nippits that actually compresses the nipples. These prevent nipple visibility if your client is going someplace that's frigidly air-conditioned. Last, I'd include some kind of really skimpy little G-string. I'm pretty fond of Cosabella's Soire G-string and also Le Mystère. Commando makes a tiny thong that's pretty good. You should also include a brief that comes up to the waist that is cut high up on the leg, like a French-cut brief.

TAILOR MADE

As important as the cutlets and belly busters are, an experienced, reputable tailor can make anything look like a million dollars. The tailor is a stylist's greatest quick-fix weapon. And yes—all good stylists employ a tailor to alter garments to fit the bodies of their clients. You'll be doing your client a huge disservce if you think you can get away with your own tiny pin tucks.

Amal Kamoo, who has tailored almost every A-list celebrity there is, says most stylists recognize when a dress doesn't fit properly, but they don't know what exactly needs to be done to make it fit. "After I pin it, they say, 'Now it looks right.'" A good seamstress is able to find a solution for every situation. Kamoo says, "If there's a dress five sizes too small, I make it work. Sometimes I reconstruct the dress. You have to be creative to know how to fix it right." A pro like Kamoo usually alters a gown in one fitting, but if the dress needs major work, she advises having a second fitting. "A trait of a great stylist is being prepared and working ahead of time," she says.

So how do you find a talented tailor? Word of mouth. A skilled seamstress may not advertise; instead she may let her work and loyal clients serve as advertisements. Look for someone who can accommodate you, even if it's last minute. "Sometimes clients need pieces overnight, and I'll have them ready," says Kamoo. "I'm always on time and I always make sure everybody is happy with the work."

DESPERATELY SEEKING A TAILOR

When you are about to do a fitting, you need someone who can do more than just tacking and stapling fixes. It pays to find the perfect expert who will do the best job and will also be discreet and professional.

Asking around is always the best—it separates the great from the good, the bad, and the ugly. Ask stores and boutiques whom they work with for their alterations. After you have a roundup of potential candidates, hold auditions and set interviews. Ask questions: How long have you been doing this? With whom have you worked? What type of work can you do—gowns; trendy, hard to rework samples; suits; taking dresses out; shortening; hand sewing and stitching; machine sewing; reworking custom tailor pockets, zippers, et cetera? Zero in on how they work with velvet, transparent fabric, embroidery, and beading. You must be able to see their previous work, so inquire if he or she keeps a book of past looks that you can review, or tailored samples that he or she can submit. Finally, ask: What hours do you keep or are you willing to keep? How long should I expect to wait before the work is done? Are you willing to collaborate? Can I have a list of references? (And when you speak to

Allure's prop kit

references, definitely ask how the collaborative process was with the tailor.)

And then, after you've settled all of the above, inquire about pricing. This is the hardest question to ask, but a very important one. Do not just let it go and be free about it. This type of work is very costly, so establish this conversation up front.

You want to go with someone who has a stellar reputation and repeat clients. If your tailor has done only a job or two with other stylists, do not make yourself the guinea pig. Go with someone who sees your vision, can work on an intense project, and can commit to crazy hours. You can do your search online, but don't get drawn in based on the celebrities with whom they've worked. You must interview, and you must call references—do not rely on e-mail. You need to hear mood and emotion from the person you're calling to figure out how your tailor affected this person. You simply don't have the time, cash, or energy to play around.

Does the stylist pay the tailor? All depends on the job. Stylist Lindsay Albanese tells me, "I always bring that expense up before I take the job." If you're doing a private client, the client pays. If it's for a show or an event, the show foots the bill and it's part of the budget.

TAILOR TO THE RESCUE

ONE OF MY FAVORITE RED CARPET DISASTER-WITH-A-SOLUTION STORIES comes from a pal who was working with the designer Roland Mouret. One of her first jobs was accompanying Scarlett Johansson to her first awards show in a dress designed by my friend's boss, Roland Mouret, for the Golden Globe Awards in 2005. The dress was not specifically designed for the celebrity, as very few new actresses have dresses custom-made for them. The stylist was not present, so my friend went to the hotel to zip her into the dress. As the actress was getting into the car, the dress completely ripped, exposing her entire backside!

A kindly neighbor brought over a mini sewing kit and tried to make minor repairs, but the color of the dress didn't match the color of the thread, so a tailor was called. Luckily there was enough time to resew the dress in the car on the way to the event. The tailor stayed to meet the actress at the end of the carpet so that she could touch up the stitching enough to endure the walk to the actress's seat and through the entire awards show. (The actress had to literally be cut out of the dress and sewn back in when she had to use the bathroom!)

62nd Annual Golden Globes, Beverly Hilton,
Los Angeles, January 2005

Q & A WITH ELIZABETH SALTZMAN

Elizabeth Saltzman hails from the world of magazine publishing as a long-time editor and contributor at Condé Nast's Vanity Fair *and is now working in the personal styling realm.*

HOW ESSENTIAL IS TAILORING?

Any young stylist needs to know that you can't get just any tailor. You need one who knows how to work with fabric, one who knows how to work with handmade lace. You can't just cut it and suddenly make a seam. You need to know how to crochet. A tailor needs to be a serious tailor, because now, with high-definition and zoom lenses, people look for flaws.

TELL ME WHAT YOU LOVE ABOUT SEEING A LOOK COME TO LIFE ON THE CARPET.

What I love is that the person looks really beautiful, feels secure, is proud, and brings something to life, which is not just the dress but an idea. And you do kind of get that fairy godmother feel when you actually have taken a very beautiful person and made her even softer or prettier or more special or different or influential or exciting to people or cause a reaction.

The excitement comes from knowing you can help designers with their businesses and from how you can drive a trend just by saying, "Okay, everybody's doing nude. Everything's going to be skin-toned, pinky, fleshy. Everyone's doing a clean face. Well I'm going with a bright pink lipstick." And all of a sudden, you see it trickle down, or the second you tell someone to go a little bit blonder, don't wear vamp nail polish, or take the earrings off, that it's been done. Whatever it is, you get this little flash of *hallelujah.*

It's really fun to take someone who's kind of perfect like Gwyneth [Paltrow] and watch her become even more perfect in a really shockingly, healthy way. It's great to take a body and know that you can put short skirts on it and she doesn't have two little pegs. She doesn't look unhealthy at all. That's exciting. It's exciting to take someone who has taste, who has an opinion, who you can agree to disagree with.

HOW DID YOU COME TO STYLE GWYNETH AND OTHERS?

When I asked *Vanity Fair,* very luckily before the financial crisis happened, if I could accept an outside job that I was offered, Graydon [Carter, *Vanity Fair*'s editor in chief] was very cool about it and said yes.

Then a couple of prospective clients came to me and said, "Would you do something?" I said, "I'm not really a stylist. But yeah, sure, I'll do it." I just never thought of myself as a stylist. And I still don't, but I love doing it. I'm not obsessed with styling someone; I'm obsessed with people looking good. I want them to look good.

If you want to be a stylist, then you have to learn from the bottom up. You actually have to work as an assistant. You have to learn the skill, and it doesn't have to be as an assistant to Rachel Zoe. I don't care if you're dressing mannequins. Learn how to dress people and watch clothes move, or how to take a picture of someone in the dress to make sure it's not showing underwear or tape, that everything isn't visible. See what happens to the garment if it rains or what happens after riding in a car for forty-five minutes or what's going to happen when a moving camera turns on.

CHAPTER SEVEN

Fashion Crimes

Just because a superstar has access to the greatest designers and stylists doesn't mean that she always walks down the red carpet a winner. Sometimes she doesn't choose any of the seventy-five dresses hanging on the rack in her hotel room at the Four Seasons. Sometimes she decides to design her own dress. Sometimes she takes a crazy risk that doesn't translate well on the carpet. And sometimes celebs just don't use the stylists they hired.

Among the usual suspects, I've mixed in looks from the new breed of fashion ingenues and dissected each outfit to explain what did or didn't work. Hopefully you'll learn how to have a discerning eye and, whenever possible, avoid sending your client out in such a look.

FELONIES

Here is a bevy of jaw-dropping moments worthy of a citizen's arrest. Despite the outrageousness, I do applaud the boldness. Whether it was matching stonewashed denim tuxedos or a vaudevillian tutu, these celebs took fashion risks—some nailing it and some truly barking. I've invited several prominent stylists to weigh in with their own perspectives, and you'll hear from them in the following pages.

VIOLATION

Celebrity offender: Lara Flynn Boyle
Violation: Acting like a drama queen
Scene of crime: 2003 Golden Globes

Pas de *don't*. This was just plain silly—a very desperate plea for attention. A few years after Björk's infamous egg lay (see page 158 in Misdemeanors), Lara had this dress custom made by designer David Cardona, a former Richard Tyler assistant. She wanted to stand out as a prima ballerina. Michel Perry created the shoes for her. This was a huge flop because it was obviously a stunt.

Golden Globes, Beverly Hills, January 2003

VIOLATION

Celebrity offender: Paula Abdul
Violation: Looking like C-3PO from *Star Wars*
Scene of crime: 2009 Grammys

This is one of my personal favorites. It's always like a circus with Paula. Three rings, dinner and show. This getup by Basil Soda was a huge disaster. Stylist Lindsay Albanese, who dresses *Access Hollywood* host Maria Menounos, says, "This is the perfect example of how a dress can actually wear you. Shorter, petite women need to be careful of wearing too many details in a gown. The severe bouffant hair and the gown's train, detail, color, and pleating were all too overpowering for Paula's frame. A trick to remember: Have no more than two dramatic details in your whole look and leave the rest simple."

VIOLATION

Celebrity offender: Toni Braxton
Violation: Trying to re-create the magic of the Jennifer Lopez low-plunge Versace dress
Scene of crime: 2001 Grammys

Leftovers, anyone? Trying to recapture the electricity that J.Lo had generated the year before, Toni Braxton and her stylists tried their hand at the same idea. She looked like she was wearing white toilet tissue held together with a band of Swarovski crystals. Richard Tyler created this for his 2001 couture line, which is odd, since his designs are normally flawless and tailored. Yet, despite how bad this looked, she will always be remembered for it. So publicity-wise, maybe it wasn't such a bad move?

51st Grammys, Los Angeles, February 2009

43rd Grammys, February 2001

VIOLATION

Celebrity offender: Geena Davis
Violation: Folies Bergère couture
Scene of crime: 1992 Oscars

Dressing like a high-kicking French chorus girl rarely does anyone justice. The dress hiked up extremely high on the thigh and then had a long train of white satin fabric in the back. The shiny satin bodice, pearls, long white satin gloves, and velvet bow-tie tap shoes were costumey. But she made no apologizes—she told the *New York Times* in 2000, "That gown fit my concept of dressing up for evening: you should go all out, make an effort. I don't care what other people think." Vincent Boucher—who has dressed Hollywood's elite, from Teri Hatcher for Clairol and the red carpet to Kiefer Sutherland on the cover of *Rolling Stone*, plus headlined numerous fashion editorials in *Esquire*, *New York* magazine, and *Vogue*—says, "Besides dressing appropriately for an event, a woman should dress her age, because a too-silly style and way-too-young look like this only makes you look older than your years. In general, the older the woman, the simpler her clothes should be to achieve a youthful look. Geena also exhibits another fashion don't: Never wear black hose with a white dress—even if it does have black straps and bow trim!"

64th Annual Academy Awards, March 1992

VIOLATION

VIOLATION

Celebrity offender: Mariah Carey
Violation: Mimi's cleavage
Scene of crime: 2006 Golden Globes

This Chanel dress was tragic. Why? Fit, fit, fit. Her very own golden globes were spilling out all over the place; the rest of the dress was simply too tight. I don't know how many more times I can say it without sounding like a broken record, but *fit is key*. No matter how much your client is dreaming of wearing Chanel or some big name, if it doesn't fit right . . . override it—this is what you are paid to do. Albanese offers this advice: "If your client is wearing satin and you see that it's pulling in at any spot, it's too tight! Also, this slick updo was too harsh for such a revealing sexy dress. Long, soft hair would have toned this down a few notches."

Celebrity offender: Destiny's Child
Violation: Letting mama stitch up your costumes on her sewing machine
Scene of crime: 2001 Brit Awards

Mama Tina Knowles sat down at her sewing machine to make these weird pageantlike confections. The color was tacky, the fabric was too shiny, and the silhouettes were simply not flattering on the girls. Beyoncé got the diva gown (of course), Michelle got something that looks very Versace-meets-Mandee, and Kelly was all covered up in a hideous jumpsuit, which is not a good cut for anyone.

Kelly Rowland, Beyoncé, Michelle Williams, Brit Awards, London, 2001

63rd Annual Golden Globes, Beverly Hilton, January 2006

VIOLATION

Celebrity offender: Kirsten Dunst
Violation: Being swallowed by gown
Scene of crime: Met Ball 2007

You know, just because this is Vintage YSL does not guarantee it's going to work. The volume was overwhelming on her frame. The shape of the gown was tentlike. It's always nice to see a good body when you have one. Sure, this was a costume ball, but nevertheless it looked like a hot, tafetta mess. Her accessories were well chosen, but she still couldn't make it work. The theme of the evening was Paul Poiret.

Kirsten Dunst and Johnny Borrell, Costume Institute Gala, New York, May 2007

VIOLATION

Celebrity offender: Macy Gray
Violation: Hires a stylist, but decides to wear this
Scene of crime: 2001 MTV Video Music Awards

On the evening of her Grammy walk she decided to ignore the fresh styling of June Ambrose, whom she had hired, and instead walked in with this creation. "My New Album Drops September 18, 2001" was the theme. When something like this happens, the celebrity usually gets tons of press for dressing like a freak, but then they have a hard time crawling out from under that rock. She topped off her gown with a flower-patterned bathing cap hat. At least she didn't have to worry about anyone else wearing that dress.

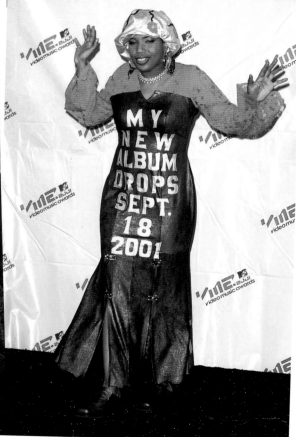

MTV Video Music Awards, September 7, 2001

1999 Academy Awards, Los Angeles

Celebrity offender: Céline Dion
Violation: Wearing a Christian Dior by John Galliano suit backward, with a dopey Stephen Jones hat and Ray-Ban sunglasses
Scene of crime: 1999 Oscars

What a Kris Kross couture mess. I had seen this on the Christian Dior runway in Paris, where it was quite a striking fashion statement. But on Céline, the runway didn't translate to the red carpet. She added the crazy white hat by Stephen Jones for Christian Dior—a complete no-no on the Oscar red carpet. No one wears hats! To make everyone even more nuts, she wore $25,000 diamond-studded Ray-Bans so no one could see her eyes! Why? She told *People* magazine: "Ray-Ban said if I wore these they would give $50,000 to my cystic fibrosis charity, so you better believe I wore them." Her stylist, Annie L. Horth, told *Entertainment Weekly* online, "She really did it for the good cause. But I wish I could have given $50,000 for her not to wear those glasses. They looked pretty ridiculous." Boucher agrees this was another couture misstep: "It was a case of dressing way too literally. The backward tuxedo is nearly impossible to pull off, though maybe with simple hair and a beautiful pair of diamond earrings she might have passed muster. But add a theatrical white fedora and suddenly it's a Vegas costume. Don't wear your sunglasses at night. Even if they're jeweled."

VIOLATION

Celebrity offender: Kate Hudson
Violation: Looking at too many old pictures of her mom, Goldie Hawn
Scene of crime: 2001 Oscars

Do not get me wrong. I am obsessed with Stella McCartney and loved her collections for Chloe. But on Kate, this vintage-style dress looked so old fashioned and weird. It reminded me of a walking lampshade. The permlike hair was a disaster and, paired with the dress, aged her. Boucher says: "What went wrong here was that Kate overdid the vintage effects. It's one thing to add one touch to an ensemble—the easiest is probably a piece of jewelry or an heirloom handbag if it's the right shape for the occasion—but here there were so many vintage elements that she looked like an extra from a Mack Sennet movie: the corkscrew curls, the fringed bolero with its arch high collar, the musty blue color, and the vintage purse that looked like it belonged at a crafts bazaar. To compound the damage, there was also a modern pitfall—the visible panty. At the very least, always stand in front of a strong light before you leave the house if you have any doubts about the coverage of the dress you are wearing."

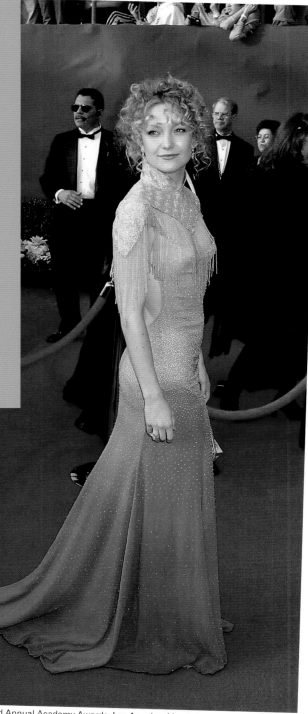

73rd Annual Academy Awards, Los Angeles, March 2001

VIOLATION

Celebrity offender: Faith Hill
Violation: Rainbow Bright in Versace
Scene of crime: 2002 Oscars

Oy. What kind of friends and family let you leave the house looking like a snow cone? Faith was coming off a stellar run of amazing looks ranging from Calvin Klein to Tom Ford for Gucci. She had transformed from a great country singer to an all-out star. But all that work went down the drain here. The satin dyed sandals look like prom Dyeables, and they didn't work with the dress. She must have wised up to her fashion foible, as she changed into a black gown as soon as she could.

VIOLATION

Celebrity offender: Alicia Keys
Violation: Ten pounds of glitter on each eyelid and a runway look that didn't work on a curvy girl
Scene of crime: 2002 Grammy Awards

She won awards at the Grammys that night, but this Christian Dior look didn't work on her. The dress wasn't fitted to her body. Keys's face was hidden in teal chiffon and embroidery. She looked uncomfortable, like she was wondering, "How can I play the piano when I've got pounds of glitter on my eyes?" Albanese agrees: "You can wear a look from the runway, but it needs to be tailored. Alicia should have nixed the boy beater and jeans and just lined the whole frock and worn it as a dress *without* that headdress. As is, it's way too costumey and theatrical. If you want your look to be ethnic inspired, wear accent pieces like a blouse or scarf."

74th Annual Academy Awards, Hollywood, CA, 2002

2002 Grammys, Los Angeles

VIOLATION

Celebrity offender: Jennifer Lopez
Violation: Hat attack!
Scene of crime: Red carpets in 2004, 2006, and 2008

Here's some Grey Gardens insanity. You have to hand it to her. J.Lo loves to take risks, especially with the dressings on her head. I applaud the "I don't give a flip what you think, I'm J.Lo" attitude, but there are times when those insane hats completely ruin what could've been a great moment. She consistently gets panned for her hats, yet continues to wear them. Stylist Neil Rodgers says, "The bottom line with hats is that you either suit them or, like the vast majority of people, you don't."

2006 MTV Video Music Awards, August 2006

MTV Music Awards, Miami, August 2004

Book launch event in New York, 2008

VIOLATION

Celebrity offender: Jennifer Hudson
Violation: Listening to *Vogue*'s André Leon Talley's advice and leaving that cropped jacket on
Scene of crime: 2007 Oscars

We were all dying to see what Academy Award hopeful Jennifer Hudson was going to wear. And we were all aghast when she arrived with her hands in the pockets of a brown Oscar de la Renta maxi gown and a too-tight gold snakeskin bolero. The shape was bad for her. The proportion of the exotic bolero jacket cut off her neck. Apparently she took guidance not from her hired stylist, Jessica Paster (who had stunning Roberto Cavalli and Michael Kors custom-made gowns waiting for her; see also her interview on page 18), but from André Leon Talley, the *Vogue* fashionista. Maybe he could have saved her if she removed the jacket. But it didn't end there. Her winged-out hair was too structured and competed with the collar of the bolero. And adding drop earrings, plus a gold necklace, was too much. Stylist Jonny Lichtenstein says this was a classic example of a stylist imposing his/her style on a fresh, young celebrity. "I think she learned from this mistake and has not looked back. She looks more comfortable in her body now, and I guarantee she will not make such a huge faux pas like that again. Runway to realway failed miserably here."

2007 Academy Awards, Hollywood, CA

Celebrity offender: Uma Thurman
Violation: Dressing like a swashbuckling Swiss Miss
Scene of crime: 2004 Oscars

Yowza! Uma, Ina, Oona . . . who are you? Where are you? Whoever kidnapped the usually stellar-dressed star needs to return her immediately. The actress, who nearly a decade earlier ushered in the era of wearing a designer gown off the rack when she announced on the red carpet that her simple, empire lilac dress was Prada, seems to have gone a bit mad in this Christian Lacroix haute couture dress. Sometimes the runway looks need to stay on the runway. Or at least be adapted to look more modern. Boucher agrees: "I went back to see how the dress was originally presented on the Lacroix couture runway, and this was no doubt a compli-cated design that should have been streamlined for life off the catwalk. In this look she's part pirate, gypsy, Greek, fräulein, Swiss Miss, and maybe a little Barbara Eden from *I Dream of Jeannie*. She looks ready to cross her arms and blink her eyes. Too bad she couldn't make it all just disappear! The blond updo only adds to the Swiss Miss effect. But from looking at the runway picture, I also real-ized something else—these voluminous layers of fabric dwarfed Uma's frame; even though she's tall, the runway model the dress was 'built' on was a lot taller and apparently skinnier. Uma left the dress semiopen, adding to the bed-worthy effect. The takeaway: You have to be a stickler about the way a dress fits. If the cut is wrong for your body, no matter how you style it, it won't work."

76th Annual Academy Awards, Hollywood, CA, February 2004

Celebrity offender: Christina Aguilera
Violation: The photo speaks for itself
Scene of crime: 2001 Grammy Awards

"Christina Aguilera had a nice idea to "be unafraid and to experiment," but when you're on the red carpet there's not much room for experimenting. Experiment on your free time when you can decide if it works. When it comes to wearing something a little bit more sexy or edgy, the Grammys are a little looser and more fun than the Golden Globes or the Oscars. But people still want to see something beautiful and sexy—not trashy. Forget the faux J.Lo and the Bo Derek hair. Christina is a beautiful woman. She can be edgy without going this far. I think she has finally found her place. Everyone makes mistakes and hopefully this is her last one." —*Stylist Ann Caruso*

Grammys, Los Angeles, February 2001

Celebrity offenders: Britney Spears, Justin Timberlake
Violation: Double denim suiting
Scene of crime: 2001 American Music Awards

His and hers matching washed denim: I would like to know who thought this was a cute idea. It will go down forever as one of the worst looks. This was trailer chic at its best. The bustier dress was custom tailored, and his jacket, jeans, and hat were made to match. Neil Rodgers says: "I think the concept of matching outfits is never a good idea. My other issues with this look were that it was denim, and a bad wash at that, had unfinished hems on Brit's dress, had patchwork, had a matching hat—I mean the list goes on and on. The whole effect was cheap and not so cheerful."

28th Annual American Music Awards, Los Angeles, January 2001

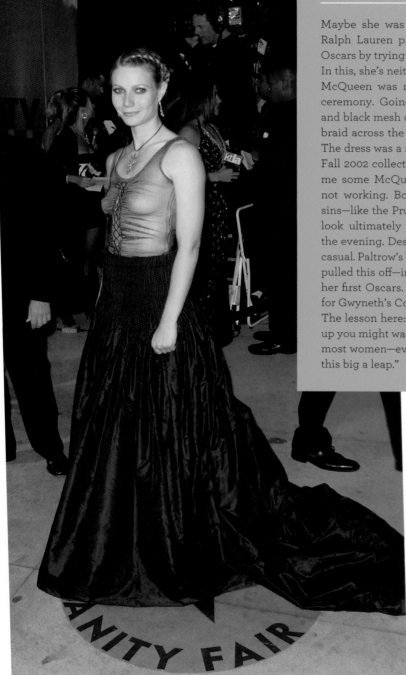

Vanity Fair Oscar Party, 2002

Celebrity offender: Gwyneth Paltrow
Violation: Goth-trosity!
Scene of crime: 2002 Oscars

Maybe she was trying to compensate for the Ralph Lauren pink dress disaster at the 1999 Oscars by trying to exude a "cool" or "dark" look. In this, she's neither. Her see-through Alexander McQueen was not appropriate for an awards ceremony. Going braless under the flesh-tone and black mesh overlay, and then adding a tight braid across the head, made this a bizarre look. The dress was a runway look from the McQueen Fall 2002 collection. Don't get me wrong! I love me some McQueen, but the execution here is not working. Boucher says: "Among its other sins—like the Prussian princess braid updo—the look ultimately just wasn't dressy enough for the evening. Despite all the jewels, it looked too casual. Paltrow's buddy Madonna just might have pulled this off—in fact she wore a similar look to her first Oscars. But it was just too far a stretch for Gwyneth's Connecticut-cum-Malibu persona. The lesson here: Know yourself. When dressing up you might want to change your style a bit, but most women—even famous ones—can't carry off this big a leap."

THE MYSTERY OF A DRESS

AS LOVELY AS THE PINK RALPH LAUREN DRESS WAS, it just didn't fit, which became apparent as Gwyneth Paltrow walked the carpet. Why would any stylist put an Oscar contender in a gown that doesn't fit? There are a lot of stories about how this dress ended up on her back. At the time, Gwyneth and Calvin Klein were pals. He'd been dressing her for endless appearances and red carpets, and even decorating living spaces for the star. It was just assumed she'd wear Calvin Klein on the red carpet. Of course, every actress reserves the right to change her mind for her big red carpet walk. But people were genuinely shocked when she arrived in Ralph and not Calvin.

Some claim that she was given $1,000,000 to wear the pink dress and it was so last minute that the dress had not been properly altered to fit. Another story has it that the in-house publicity department called Gwyneth at Ralph Lauren's insistence and asked her to wear the dress as a personal favor. Gwyneth and her camp have stayed mum on the topic, so the mystery will likely never be revealed.

Meanwhile, what gets everyone's knickers in a twist is that the dress didn't even fit right. It grew like a Chia Pet as she walked the carpet. Apparently she had removed the breast pads in the dress, making it not sit properly.

71st Annual Academy Awards, winner
Oscar for Best Actress, March 1999

MISDEMEANORS

Here are my picks of the pans. These looks were widely loathed, but I can't help but respect these ladies for taking fashion risks.

VIOLATION

Celebrity offender: Katie Holmes
Violation: Are those Tom's jeans she's wearing?
Scene of crime: Streets of Manhattan, August 2008

Katie Holmes had never been considered a maker of fashion trends, but in 2008, when she was in New York rehearsing for a play and would leave her home every day wearing baggy denim jeans by Prps (friend Victoria Beckham was wearing the same jeans at the same time), she launched a huge trend: the Boyfriend Jean. At first everyone assumed these jeans were Tom Couch-Jumping Cruise's. She wore them with flat Mary Janes or Azzedine Alaïa heels, oversize boyfriend cardigans or leather jackets, Chloe bags, and H&M scarves. I will never forget how bad my coworkers thought the look was. But slowly celebrities like Reese Witherspoon, Heidi Klum, and Rachel Bilson followed. And it's still with us. She ushered in a movement and a trend. Albanese concurs: "Women initially gawked at this trend because it was very masculine and a bit sloppy. What turned our opinion around was the fact that this was very easy street chic—and comfortable when worn the right way. The key? Pairing form-fitting basics on top to show you have shape."

New York, August 2008

Celebrity offender: Beyoncé
Violation: Trying to show her edgy side
Scene of crime: 2008 MTV Europe Awards

The Space Invaders dress just doesn't seem like something that Beyoncé really understands. I love love love that Beyoncé ditched mom's House of Deréon for once and went in another direction to show just how badass she is. Her sister Solange introduced her to the designer Gareth Pugh. There was some scuttlebutt that this dress was in response to the edgy allure that the younger Rihanna brings. Rodgers says: "I actually think this outfit would have worked for an onstage musical performance. The thing is that we're not used to seeing Beyoncé so covered up. It was a bold fashion choice, however; the metal glove was the perfect accessory for this futuristic look, and the hair and makeup tied the whole modern, sleek look together."

MTV Europe Music Awards, Liverpool, England, November 2008

Celebrity offender: Rose McGowan
Violation: Nudist retreat
Scene of crime: 1998 MTV Video Music Awards

What the hell was she thinking? She was wearing decorative floss: Nude sequins, no bra, leopard G-string. It was an attention grabber. I didn't know whether to applaud or barf. Lichtenstein adds: "Bad taste as it was, this dress put her on the map! She will forever be known for this event, this dress, and this moment. She knew *exactly* what she was doing here, and it worked. She separated herself from Manson as an image."

Rose McGowan and Marilyn Manson,
MTV Music Awards, Los Angeles, 1998

VIOLATION

Celebrity offender: Björk
Violation: Wearing Marjan Pejoski's swan dress
Scene of crime: 2001 Oscars

Ah . . . this was the dress that literally laid an egg. It was panned. Laughed at. Yet, it might be one of my favorite looks of all time. Why? She's an artist. She took a chance. She had been nominated for a song in the movie *Dancer in the Dark*. As she arrived with the swan around her neck, she was dropping eggs as she walked. She explained: "Well, I did bring eggs. Six of them that I left all over the red carpet. Come on, you don't bring eggs unless you want to take the piss, right?" She continued, "I was actually amazed at how many people thought I was serious. I didn't mean to cause a riot. It was really funny because the security guards would pick them up and run after me with their walkie-talkies saying, 'Excuse me, miss, you dropped this.'" As mad as a hatter as she is, I have to admire her for having worn it. Can you imagine packing this box for FedEx, eggs and all? She paired her swanlike dress with sparkled hose and must-have Balenciaga white heels. The good news? She donated the dress to be auctioned off at an Oxfam benefit. Stylist Neil Rodgers reminds us, "The thing with Björk is that she is a hugely successful musician from Iceland, not a movie or TV actress, and is renowned for her avant-garde fashion statements, generally quirky behavior, and beautiful, unusual music. I think she just wanted to have fun with this outfit. It was designed by her friend and long-term collaborator Marjan Pejoski, whose spring '01 collection was bird themed. Therefore the point was to be loyal to Marjan, create some publicity, and have some fun while doing it. An unconventional success!"

73rd Annual Academy Awards, Los Angeles, March 2001

VIOLATION

Celebrity offender: First Lady Michelle Obama
Violation: Somebody call 911! This dress is on fire!
Scene of crime: Election night, Chicago, Illinois, November 5, 2008

Some people absolutely loved Michelle Obama's fearless dress by Narciso Rodriguez. Yet many hated it. Love it or hate it, this dress, with its wool treatment in red over the black satin, signified the change the Obamas were talking about—it was new, fresh, unexpected, unconventional, and a huge fashion risk. Another thing? She wore an American designer. Who else could've done this and pulled it off? The cummerbund belt was fabulously risqué, sexy, and a total envelope-pusher. We couldn't wait to see what she would do next. This will be four fabulous years of nonstop fashion to covet, blog, and obsess over. Lichtenstein agrees: "I think she wanted to break all molds of what the first lady was supposed to wear. She wanted to show the world: I am young, energetic, and not afraid of taking a risk."

Chicago, November 2008

VIOLATION

Celebrity offender: Sarah Jessica Parker
Violation: Complete coutorture
Scene of crime: AngloMania Costume Institute Gala at the Metropolitan Museum of Art, May, 2006

There were a lot of headshakers out there with this look, but what was kind of fabulous was that she dressed spot-on for the annual costume ball. The critics objected to the plaid layered and belted over the gorgeous lace dress. I liked it because it was completely eccentric. She was playing with the fashion theme of AngloMania. She was the late Alexander McQueen's date, and as heinous and hideous as people and bloggers thought they looked, I think they dressed the part.

Costume Institute Ball, New York, May 2006

MTV Movie Awards, Los Angeles, May 2009

VIOLATION

Celebrity offender: Kristen Stewart
Violation: Chuck Taylors on the red carpet
Scene of crime: MTV Movie Awards, May 2009

Another great moment that had many haters. K-Stew wore Converse Chuck Taylors with her Yigal Azrouël red-and-black taffeta dress on the carpet. Isn't that a young and groovy thing to do? And something a tad different? Apparently, she had a twisted ankle and it wasn't possible to schlep up and down the carpet in a stiletto heel. As one of the stars of the *Twilight* juggernaut, she made a modern, what-the-cool-girls-want-to-wear statement at the MTV Movie Awards—and isn't this the place, the event where you can bend and stretch the rules? Albanese agrees: "This worked because the dress was funky, edgy, and hit right at her thigh, making her legs look long and lean, even with Chucks on! The trick is to keep accessories minimal when trying to rock this trend. Edgier rock-and-roll dresses in darker colors work best. Never wear with pastel, silk, chiffon, or satin dresses. I promise it won't work!"

LADIES AND GENTLEMEN... MEET YOUR FUTURE CLIENTS

Clockwise from left top: Mercy James, New York, February 20, 2010 / Suri Cruise, on set of *Son of No One*, Bronx, New York, April 12, 2010 / Lourdes Ciccone, 2nd Annual Bent on Learning Benefit, New York, April 28, 2010 / Valentina Hayek Pinault, Beverly Center, Los Angeles, December 31, 2009 / Harlow Madden, Coffee Bean and Tea Leaf after leaving Fit for Kids, Los Angeles, March 2010 / Honor Warren, Beverly Hills, March 17, 2010 / Kingston Rossdale, Beverly Hills, April 2010 / Shiloh and Zahara Jolie-Pitt, France, October 2009

EDU-MA-CATE ME!

It pays to understand the lingo. Here's a brief glossary of terms and phrases you'll hear in the styling biz:

*$: Abbreviation for Starbucks.

-AGE: A slang suffix to make a word sound much cooler. For instance, *boob-age, Stefani-age.*

BBL: abbreviation for *be back later.*

BESPOKE: A fancy way to describe something custom made.

BIAS CUT: A cut that runs in a diagonal and against the grain of the fabric. This cut is very popular in modern bridal dresses and evening wear. Originally developed by Madeleine Vionnet, Edith Head brought the technique into vogue in early Hollywood. Bias-cut garments drape beautifully. In the 1920s and '30s Jean Harlow wore only bias-cut gowns. It became her trademark.

BODY-CON: Short for *body conscious,* if you're too tired, darling, to say all four syllables. Your boss or coworker may believe it means *body contour* or *body control*—both are fine and really not worth a huge argument.

BTW: Abbreviation for *by the way.*

CHAMOIS: It's not pronounced like the ShamWow on TV. It's pronounced *shamee.* And it's a yellowish-hued leather from a chamois goat.

-CHIC: Used as a suffix. *Chic* of course is something that's very classy, sophisticated, and glamorous. There's boho-chic (part bohemian, folksy, chic, and understated), heroin-chic (referencing a time in the 1990s when everyone dressed like they were chicly strung out), hobo-chic, indie-chic, rebel-chic, agro-chic, geek-chic, shabby-chic, über-chic . . . the list goes on and on.

CHICKEN CUTLET OR CUTLET: A silicone breast enhancer that's inserted into a bodice of a dress. When your client needs some extra help to fill out her dress, this item is your best friend.

CHICONOMICS: Something that's chic and remains strong through a recession or economic meltdown.

COMBO NAMES: I kind of hate these mashed-together terms, such as *jeggings*—leggings that look like jeans; *skapris*—a skirt and capri pants combined; *shants*—sheer pants; *bandals*—boot sandals; *shress*—sheer dress.

DÉCOLLETÉ: This is a deep neckline that reveals cleavage, neck, and shoulders.

DIAMANTE: Fake jewels and decoration; rhinestones that imitate diamonds. Fashion people always use this term and most people just say, "Huh?" But it sounds superfancy. Again, roll with it.

DIAPHANOUS: You may hear something like, "Find me something more *diaphanous.*" I remember when I heard this one and I was like, whaaaaaaa? It generally means a delicate and refined fabric such as tissue chiffon.

DIRECTIONAL: Something that's very current and trendy and fashion forward.

EDGY: I actually hate this word. It's used to describe something that's trendy yet dark and cool. When I was at *Seventeen* magazine, we weren't "edgy enough." Ugh.

EDITRIX: A top editor at a glossy magazine.

EMPIRE: This is a tricky one. You can either say *empire,* like the Empire State Building, or *om-peer.* Fashion people do both. But basically, it's a cut that was named after Empress Joséphine, who wore the style during the French Napoleonic empire in silk, chiffon, and velvet. It features a skirt that gathers underneath the breasts, with a low neckline and a poufed sleeve. This style is timeless and will never, ever go away.

EXOTI-RICAN: Coined by Paul Cavaco, my old boss, it describes someone who has an exotic look.

GHETTO FABULOUS: Wearing one's wealth. The roots of this phrase lie in hip-hop, originally used to describe someone from the 'hood who buys expensive things such as bling, cars, and the hottest designer goods. John Galliano for Dior created an entire collection based around *ghetto fabulous* fashion. It looks like streetwear from the 'hood, but wealthy people pay oodles of dollars for it.

GHETTO-IZATION: A term used to describe when mainstream fashion and style has a strong element or influence of hip-hop or rap culture and the "-ization" makes it worldly. See also, "Sooo *ghetto*."

HAUTE COUTURE: This is another tough French thing to say. But it's pronounced like *oat coot-tour*. These are garments made to order for clients. These pieces are not mass produced and may only see the light of day with one very wealthy client. Also, know that an actual couture designer must be certified by a specific group in France, so things that are one-of-a-kind are not necessarily couture.

"I'M HAVING A _____ MOMENT": When you hear this, it means the speaker is obsessing over a time period or a look or a style, and he or she wants to create a story or a look based on this thought. For instance, "I'm having a *Days of Heaven* moment," means prairie chic. Or "I'm having a Stevie moment" means gypsy bohemian à la Stevie Nicks.

"I'M THINKING . . .": Similar to the "I'm having a _____ moment," this sort of statement means that the speaker has a very specific visual in mind. In the case of "I'm thinking . . . Ann-Margret on a bike," the stylist is referencing a visual of the actress Ann-Margret, a '60s and '70s icon, on a bike. Her hair and makeup will probably have a very specific direction, as well as her clothing. Use these sorts of references as a starting point to put the look in context.

-ISH: A suffix used to indicate a type. For instance, *insider-ish*, *red carpet-ish*.

"IT'S SCREAMING _____": This is the statement that a dress, a look, or an outfit makes. For instance, "It's screaming Elvira!"

"IT'S VERY AUDREY": There are oh-so-many great Audrey Hepburn looks from movies such as *Sabrina*, *Breakfast at Tiffany's*, *My Fair Lady*, and *Funny Face*. Is it the perfect little black dresses, statement jewelry, the "Joséphine" empire white dress, black silk dupioni dresses, trench coats, and chunky highlights in the hair, black turtlenecks, or black pants and loafers? The answer is always yes. You can never have too much Audrey.

JACKIE O.: When you hear a reference to Jackie, always ask if the speaker means Jacqueline Bouvier, Jacqueline Kennedy, or Jacqueline Kennedy Onassis. Meaning: You need to know if your boss is referencing when Jackie was a *Life* photographer, horsewoman pre–White House, First Lady, or when she went to Greece and married Aristotle Onassis. It's the same woman, but she had so many amazing, iconic looks in her many incarnations.

LOL: Abbreviation for *laughing out loud*.

"MAKE IT MORE MODERN": Here's an example of how this may be used: "I would love Michelle Pfeiffer in the Prada giving me 'Swedish' but *make it more modern*." Oy. This took me a while to figure out too, but it actually makes sense. It means that the idea is based on a collection (Prada) that has a folkloric (Swedish) flavor but needs to change up and become very modern for the times . . . meaning: changing the hair or the lipstick or the bag to make it feel more current. Every collection you see has a reference, and your boss will know that. Yes, sometimes it will seem ridiculous—but just roll with it.

MASCULINE/FEMININE: This term generally means womenswear that looks like menswear but is not actually made for a man. For instance, a "boyfriend" blazer, a crisp white shirt, vest, tie, and trousers. For a visual reference, check out *Annie Hall* or anything designed by Ralph Lauren.

MORE OPTIONS: This means more dresses, more jewelry, more everything.

MOVIE REFERENCES: Stylists will often drop a movie name or a scene, and you're expected to know exactly what they're referencing and call in clothing that has that look. For instance, "You know that moment in *Gloria* when Gena Rowlands is walking down the street in the Bronx and the wind is blowing in her hair? That's the look that we want for our girl." You have no idea what that means? Rent the movie immediately, find it on YouTube, or Google it quick. Then you'll know that this means a great camel cashmere coat with a beautiful pump over a blouse and pencil skirt. Other common movie references: *They Shoot Horses Don't They?*, *9½ Weeks*, *Mahogany*, *Bonnie and Clyde*, *Grey Gardens*, *Valley of the Dolls*, *Network*, *Flashdance*, *Fame*, *West Side Story*, *Gypsy*, *Viva Las Vegas*.

MUFFIN TOP: When the midriff pours over a waistband.

OMG: Abbreviation for *Oh, my God.*

ON TREND: Another way of saying *trendy.*

OOC: Abbreviation for *out of control.*

OTT: Abbreviation for *over the top.*

OY GEVALT!: Yiddish for *surprise!* Everyone in fashion uses Yiddish as a second language. Doesn't matter if you aren't a scholar or Jewish—it's the universal language of fashion. See also, *Oy vey.*

OY VEY: From *Oy vey iz mir,* a Yiddish expression that translates to *Oh, woe is me.* But you don't have to be Jewish to use this . . . everyone in fashion does.

PAS POSSIBLE: I love it when a non-bilingual individual will suddenly start speaking in French when something goes wrong. "This gown is *pas possible,*" meaning not possible!

"A REAL WOMAN": This phrase makes me mental. You'll hear it used to describe a female who isn't a celebrity, a model, or an actress.

ROCK: A way of saying *wear,* as in: "She could totally *rock* that look."

RUCHING: A crimp or pleat on a lace or chiffon. Pronounced *rooshing.*

SHAHTOOSH: A Persian scarf woven with the down hair of antelope. They're expensive and very precious, and banned in America, China, and India.

SHE OWNS IT: A look made for a particular person that no one else could pull off.

THE SHUT-UP HUT: One of many ways to say *stop it.* There's also *shut up, shut it down, shut the front door, shut it off,* and *stop because you are killing me with your fierceness.*

"SOOO GHETTO!": This means something appears chintzy or trashy. But it can also be turned around and used to mean that it's cool to act poor.

STATEMENT NECKLACE/PIECE: This is a huge piece of jewelry that can be the centerpiece of a look.

TBW: Abbreviation for *to be worn.*

TDF: Abbreviation for *to die for.*

"THIS IS GIVING ME _____": This phrase is used when you look at something that reminds you of something else or something that feels familiar. For instance, "This is giving me Anna Sui circa 1998."

TOTES!: Meaning "Totally! Yes! Doing it! Done!" *Def* can be added to reconfirm that you're totally, definitely on top of the situation, as in *totes def!*

RESOURCES

Who do you call when you need haute couture delivered same day or overnight? Where do you go for last-minute alterations? Who makes the house call on an awards night? Where can you get a vintage dress reworked? Here you'll find the ultimate insider's list from stylists who have opened their little black books for me.

You'll also discover my favorite fashion and style Web sites and blogs. I check these on a daily basis so I can keep up. You can print out magazine editorial pages without spending a mint and also get a global view of what's being editorialized. There are sites that highlight amazing street style that you can study and reinterpret. You can also find some postings for job opportunities as well as sites that show the latest trends on the red carpet and on the street, and what's selling or on wait lists.

GARMENT CLEANING AND REPAIR

DRY CLEANERS
Kelly Ripa, talk show hostess and actress, is a huge fan of Madame Paulette Cleaners in New York. The company specializes in handling luxe designer and haute couture pieces with beading or embroidery. It's able to remove the most stubborn stains from gowns and garments. The firm has worked with all the major fashion houses and designers for more than a half century, and it's always finding new ways to expand its services, which now extend to home furnishings maintenance. *www.madamepaulette.com; (347) 689-7010; 1255 2nd Ave., New York, New York 10065*

L.A. designers depend on Four Seasons Cleaners. Fscleaners.com; (323) 848-9158; 8042 Santa Monica Blvd., West Hollywood, California, 90046-5009

FUR CLEANING AND REPAIR
Pologeorgis Furs can remodel granny's chinchilla bathrobe coat into a cropped chubbie. It also cleans shearling-, leather-, and fur-lined garments. If you're slammed for time, the company picks up in Manhattan. *www.polo georgis.com; (212) 563-2250; 143 West 29th St., New York, New York 10001*

KNIT REPAIR
Alter Knit is the ultimate place to have your fine knits restored to their best possible condition. The experts there can repair moth holes, adjust body length, change hems, shorten sleeves, and redesign necklines. There are also cleaning specialists on hand for quick touch-ups and de-pilling. You can even design and customize your own knitwear with them via e-mail. If you're outside NYC, no problem. Just fill out the online form and mail it with your items. *www.alterknitnewyork.com; (212) 387-0707; 192 Lexington Ave., 2nd floor, New York, New York 10016*

GEAR

GARMENT BAGS
You're going to need all sorts of gear for returning clothing: plain brown bag shopping bags in all sizes, tissue paper, and garment bags. Stylist Vincent Boucher recommends Travel Auto Bag Co. in New York. It carries fold-over suit and dress garment bags, canvas breathing bags, and deluxe rack covers to protect an entire rolling rack. *www .travelautobag.com; (212) 840-0025; 264 W. 40th St., New York, New York 10018*

RACKS
You're going to need clothing racks to do your schlepping and for hanging your clothes. I go to ClothesRacks.com for one-stop shopping for industrial racks, garment bags, and hangers. It stocks heavy-duty, collapsible, single-rail, double-rail, split-rail, and other types of racks. Each rack can hold up to 500 pounds of load capacity. *www .clothesracks.com; (877) 637-3711*

MAKEUP

Somalian-born übermodel Iman has a Web site that rocks (makeup galore for women of all colors, plus jewelry and a blog); a successful line of accessories called Iman Global Chic on HSN.com that features shoes, bags, and carry-on luggage for everyone; and she's married to one of the most inspirational musicians of the twentieth century. Mrs. David Bowie launched her personal Web site in 2005, her lifestyle line on HSN in 2007, and she's not slowing down. Read her blog for amazing behind-the-scenes tips from leading makeup artists and stylists, plus cosmetics how-tos and makeovers. www.imancosmetics.com and www.hsn.com

MISCELLANEOUS

EMBELLISHMENTS

M&J Trimming is one of the best places to get beads, baubles, rhinestones, and notions. Its 5,000-square-foot showroom is teeming with ribbons from France, laces from Switzerland, Austrian Swarovski crystals, and buttons from Italy, plus an array of tassels, patches, studs, nailheads, and idea boards. If you can't make it to the store, check out its massive Web site. Clients range from Macy's to Victoria's Secret to Vera Wang. www.mjtrim.com; (800) 965-8746 or (212) 204-9595; 1008 6th Ave., New York, New York 10018

PROP KIT ESSENTIALS

Blair Levin, who works with Mariah Carey, tells me that the best way to prevent spilling out of a dress is to use TopStick—clear double-sided adhesive strips made to hold hairpieces to the scalp. Load up on these. TopStick now makes Fashion Fix apparel and body tape to secure plunging necklines, hold up strapless tops, keep bra straps in place, and temporarily hem a pant. www.fashionfixtape.com; (800) 443-8856

RESEARCH AND REFERENCING

One of my favorite places to look at tons of pictures, advertisements, and old magazine tear sheets for photo research is the New York Public Library Picture Collection. It's in the Mid-Manhattan Library and is also searchable online. www.digitalgallery.nypl.org/mmpco; (917) 275-6975; 455 5th Ave., New York, New York 10016

....

WikiHow is an online how-to manual that you can edit. When I looked up how to press a shirt, I found not only a great tip list, but also options to discuss the topic, edit, and watch a video to learn how to do it! www.wikihow.com

....

YouTube is where you can find clips of all sorts. A few of my favorites for you to research:

- Elsa Klensch, who covered everything and everyone in fashion in the 1980s
- The Thierry Mugler collection of She Devils of 1988
- The evolution of designers like Calvin Klein, Donna Karan, Ralph Lauren (being the first to go backstage and report directly from the horse's mouth was revolutionary back then)
- The amazing *House of Style* series (1989–2000) hosted by Cindy Crawford, Rebecca Romijn, Molly Sims, Amber Valetta, and Shalom Harlow. This series was done very slickly and beautifully, going behind the scenes on shoots with supermodels and designers and done in a younger, funkier way than CNN handled such reporting. Add music of the era and it is complete inspirational heaven. Some of the reporting feels like the girls are flatlined, and it's funny to watch, but it's the fashion and the lifestyle and the fun that they forecasted that make it all a joy to watch again, or for the first time.
- *Solid Gold*: The dance show where the guests were stellar, the dancing was phenomenal, and the clothing was sick!
- *Paper Dolls*: The made for television movie starring Daryl Hannah and Alexandra Paul with fabulous fashion, lots of model attitude, and hilariously bitchy mothers. It was later made into a star-studded TV series.
- *Mahogany*: This movie makes me mental in a great way. I love watching Diana Ross "model."
- *Love Story*: Great costumes in this movie. It's very inspiring to watch when you need ideas for a fall fashion story.
- *The Eyes of Laura Mars*: This is one of my favorite fashion movies—the photos, the music, the fashion! Streisand sings a crazy theme song. This was Faye Dunaway in her 1970s finest!

SHIPPING

In order to get your samples or clothes on time, it's essential to have a have dependable courier at your fingertips who can immediately pick up or deliver a package or carnet. I recommend Worldnet. Taylor Jacobson swears by them, as does Film Fashion, a division of the P.R. agency Rogers & Cowan, which specializes in matching fashion and accessories with celebrities to increase brand awareness. The rates are expensive, but the company prides itself on its fashion and luxury goods shipping expertise. *Worldnet-intl.com; (718) 244-5929 in New York and (310) 568-9158 in Los Angeles*

I also highly recommend Marken Worldwide Express. This courier has saved my life and job many times. It offers same-day service and speedy overseas service. *(718) 528-1800*

SHOE REPAIR

Leather Spa is the fashion industry's big secret. No job is too much for the staff—replacing heels, shaving down heel heights, fixing straps, and stretching, cleaning, and dyeing shoes. Owners Carlos and David Mesquita have more than thirty years of experience in luxury shoe repair and reconditioning. *www.leatherspa.com; (212) 262-4823; 10 W. 55th St., New York, New York 10019*

In L.A., go to Arturo's Shoe Fix *(310) 278-9585; 9643 Santa Monica Blvd., Beverly Hills, California 90210*; and Progressive Shoe Shop *(310) 276-8717; 9418 Dayton Way, Beverly Hills, California 90210.*

SPECIALTY CLOTHING

MATERNITY WEAR

Check out the maternity boutique on the Bare Necessities Web site. For nursing bras, look to the Elle Macpherson Intimates, Anita, Le Mystère, and Bravado! brands. A nursing bra does not need to be ugly. There are some beautiful ones out there. It's best, though, to avoid underwire. *www.bare necessities.com; (877) 728-9272*

Isabella Oliver offers timeless and elegant clothing with its own magazine that addresses personal styling, as well as a blog. It recommends five must-haves for maternity wear: a wrap column dress, a woolen trench, a bracelet portrait top, Marilyn jeans, and the perfect tote. The clothing is so versatile, moms can wear it postdelivery too. *www.isabellaoliver.com; (800) 961-4963*

For one-stop shopping, check out A Pea in the Pod. You'll find Nicole Richie's and Heidi Klum's lines here. The retailer also stocks Joie jeans and celebrity jersey dress favorite, Rachel Pally. You'll also find chic swimwear, evening wear, dresses, lingerie, outerwear, Spanx, and activewear. *www.apea inthepod.com; (877) 273-2763*

A few other handy sources are: Japanese Weekend, *www.japaneseweekend .com, (800) 808-0555*; Moody Mamas, *www.moodymamas.com*, from *Project Runway* winner Christian Siriano; and Veronique Maternity, *www.veronique maternity.com, (212) 831-7800*

UNDERPINNINGS

From expert bra fittings to impeccable undergarment and body-slimming service, Bra Tenders is a wonderful resource (see also Q & A with Lori Kaplan, page 138). The staff has worked with celebrities including Carrie Underwood and Kate Winslet. They are always available for costume emergencies or to do a quick fix on a wardrobe malfunction. *www.bratenders.com; (212) 957-7000 and (888) 438-2272; 630 9th Ave., Ste. 601, New York, New York 10036*

Frederick's of Hollywood—a place where you can find everything from derrière pick-me-up bands (to assist in lifting your bottom) to soaring platform footwear to liquid lifting bras—has been a California institution since 1946, when Frederick Mellinger invented the push-up bra. *www.fredericks.com; (323) 957-5953; 6751 Hollywood Blvd., Hollywood, California 90028*

Stylists and celebrities love Orchard Corset. The company stocks everything: bras, corsets, compression garments, hosiery, panties, plus-size pieces, and bridal garters. Blair Levin, who works with Mariah Carey and is the chief *American Idol* stylist, favors this shop. *www.orchardcorset.com; (212) 674-0786; 157 Orchard St., New York, New York 10002*

Since 1888, Town Shop has been one of the most famous lingerie shops on the planet. It specializes in lingerie and, most important, the fit. Cup sizes range from AAs to JJs. The retailer also carries a large array of great-fitting swimwear, hosiery, and shape- and sleepwear. *www.townshop.com; (212) 787-2762; 2273 Broadway, New York, New York 10024*

VINTAGE-CLOTHING RETAILERS

Where do stylists get those gorgeous vintage pieces? The stores listed here are not only incredible meccas for amazing pieces but also great places to ask questions and get a valuable fashion education. You can find out who designed it and learn about cuts and drapes of clothing from eras past. Listen, learn, and make new friends. Extremely helpful tip: when you travel, send a post on Facebook asking your friends where they suggest shopping for vintage in that area.

I just love the way owners Marco Liotta and Patti Bordoni edit their men's and women's merchandise. Amarcord Vintage Fashion is a fashion editor's paradise. The eras represented go from the 1940s to the 1980s. Of course, the company is named after the famous 1973 Fellini movie. It's a lovely romp through great coats, Gucci bags, and knee-high leather boots from the 1970s. www.amarcordvintagefashion.com; (212) 431-4160; 252 Lafayette St., New York, New York 10012; and (718) 963-4001, 223 Bedford Ave., Brooklyn, New York 11211

Annie Cream Cheese is owned by a cute girl named Annie Lee who actually started her business on eBay in 2001. Jessica Alba, Nicole Richie, Tory Burch, Victoria Beckham, and Daniel Craig have all shopped this store. Lee features really great vintage coats, bags, and boots. She carries vintage Missoni, Gucci, Emilio Pucci, Carlos Falchi, Charles Jourdan, and Ferragamo, to name a few. www.anniecreamcheese.com; (202) 298-5555, 3279 M St. N.W., Washington, D.C. 20007; or (702) 452-9600, 3327 Las Vegas Blvd., Las Vegas, Nevada 89109

I love C. Madeleine's because its stock includes pieces from as far back as the 1800s, with beautiful lace, waistcoats, and lingerie. Each area is sorted by decade. So after the Victorian-looking stuff, there's Norma Kamali and Thierry Mugler, then a disco explosion directly behind you. Jewelry, shoes, hats, purses, furs—it's massive. Give yourself time. There's too much to see if you just cruise in before closing. www.cmadeleines.com; (305) 945-7770; 13702 Biscayne Blvd., North Miami Beach, Florida 33181

Vintage lover, stylist, and collector Cameron Silver owns and operates Decades and Decades Two in Los Angeles. Opened in 1997, this is a haven for stylists and celebrities who love to collect vintage. Choose from '20s gowns, '70s hippie duds, and Hermès Birkins, and possibly bump into stylist Rachel Zoe while you're there. Silver knows a thing or two about vintage fashion. You can learn a lot from him on how to shop and what to collect. Check out the company's blog detailing its vast inventory and new acquisitions. www.decadesinc.com; (323) 655-0223; 8214½ Melrose Ave., Los Angeles, California 90046

Highly recommended for its awesome collection, Fly Boutique is in Miami. Who wouldn't be inspired by anything that comes from that neck of the woods? www.flyboutiquevintage.com; (305) 604-8508; 650 Lincoln Rd., South Beach, Florida 33139

Frock is where Julia Roberts bought her vintage YSL dress that she wore on the carpet of the sixty-seventh Golden Globe Awards. It was modern, very chic, different, and not gowny. www.frocknyc.com; (212) 594-5380; 170 Elizabeth St., New York, New York 10012

Gadabout Vintage is a great vintage resource. It carries everything from Oleg Cassini and Ciel Chapman (a Marilyn Monroe favorite) to church-lady hats, toys in boxes, and huge '70s sunglasses. The clothes date from the late 1800s to the 1970s and all are in excellent condition. Check out the Web site to see the YouTube video of the store. It's amazing. www.gadabout.ca; (416) 463-1254; 1300 Queen St. E., Toronto, Ontario, Canada M4L 1C4

Furniture, fashion, jewelry, shoes, boots, vintage, vintage styled, and recycled clothing can all be found at Hong Kong Vintage & Recycled. Its items are well priced and well organized. www.hongkongvintage.com; (704) 334-0538; 1514 Central Ave., Charlotte, North Carolina 28205

Opened in 1971, Rag Stock specializes in quality used clothing. It has fourteen locations from Wisconsin to Iowa and Illinois. There is very cool stuff online as well: men's, women's, kids', costumes, '80s paint-splattered sweatshirts, biker jackets, go-go boots, and more. www.ragstock.com; (612) 823-6690; 1433 W. Lake St., Minneapolis, Minnesota 55408. (763) 546-9955; 7924 Olsen Memorial Highway, Golden Valley, Minnesota 55427. (608) 251-3419; 329 State Street, Madison, Wisconsin 52730. (773) 868-9263; 812 West Belmont Ave., Chicago, Illinois 60657

Fun, funky, and fabulous fashion from every era can be found at Regal Vintage. This retailer buys and sells vintage clothing, accessories, purses, and everything under the twentieth-century umbrella. www.regalvintage.com; (303) 830-0216; 1866 S. Broadway, Denver, Colorado 80210

I love Resurrection's edit of merchandise and the way it all works together. This retailer has amazing fashion books. The clothing is properly taken care of and the store doesn't have that vintage smell. I always feel like I learn something new about a designer whenever I go in. Owner Katy Rodriguez is a delight. She has an incredible archive and knowledge about everything fashion. I also love the store's focus on one movement or designer at a time. *www.resurrectionvintage.com; (212) 625-1374, 217 Mott St., New York, New York 10012; and (323) 651-5516, 8006 Melrose Ave., Los Angeles, California 90046*

Second Run is the place where Sarah Palin got her secondhand Dolce & Gabbana pink jacket when she was running for vice president in 2008. I will never forget this place because we called it a hundred times trying to verify if other pieces of Palin's wardrobe were purchased there or at Neiman Marcus. She did buy a lot there, and it is a very nice second-run upscale resale shop in Anchorage. It resells Dolce, Juicy Couture, Chloe (when Stella McCartney was the designer), Lipstik Girls (a Suri Cruise favorite), and Marc Jacobs. *Outoftheclosetalaska.com; (907) 277-6119; 720 D St., Anchorage, Alaska, 99501*

The Way We Wore is a wonderful and beloved store with a locked-in vintage educator, owner Doris Raymond. This store houses clothing, accessories, a library with patterns, and pictures and books. Many celebrity stylists shop here for their red carpet looks: Arianne Phillips (Madonna), Rachel Zoe, Estee Stanley, Cristina Ehrlich, and Jennifer Rade (Angelina Jolie). *www.thewaywewore.com; (323) 937-0878; 334 S. La Brea Ave., Los Angeles, California 90036*

STUDIO SERVICES

Kristen Turner, a stylist in Los Angeles, told me that when she's lucky enough to have a budget to pull clothing, she goes to studio services in department stores. "You're able to get the clothes you need, but they request that you pay for a percentage of all the merchandise you take with you—it's called a *keep*. This can range anywhere from 15 to 50 percent." And you keep what you paid for. To make appointments call: Barneys New York in Beverly Hills, *(310) 276-4400*, or in NYC, *(212) 826-8900;* Bergdorf Goodman in NYC, *(212) 872-8772;* Bloomingdales at the Beverly Center in L.A., *(310) 360-2714,* in NYC, *(212) 705-3673,* or in Sherman Oaks, *(818) 325-2301;* Fred Segal on Melrose Avenue in L.A., *(323) 651-4129;* Lord & Taylor in NYC, *(212) 382-7672;* Macy's in Beverly Hills, *(310) 659-9660;* Nordstrom in L.A., *(310) 254-1670;* Saks Fifth Avenue in L.A., *(310) 271-6726,* or in NYC, *(877) 551-7257.*

STYLING

You can find all sorts of styling inspiration online. Web sites such as www.closetcouture.com and www.polyvore.com let you design entire looks by mixing and matching various clothing and accessories from online stores. Don't stop there. Almost every Web site retailer from J.Crew to Hot Topic offers styling suggestions with tabs such as: "You Might Also Like . . ." or "Shop the Look."

TAILORS

Whether you need a couture dress taken in or store-bought pants hemmed, Amal Kamoo works wonders. She's one of Hollywood's most sought-after tailors. *(818) 817-0646*

Fashion stylists and magazine editors on the East Coast flock to Lars Nord for their biggest tailoring needs. When I worked at *Allure*, we enlisted Lars to make a mirror-encrusted body stocking for Mariah Carey's "Glitter" shoot/cover, and he basically stitched that baby up overnight. Editors run over to his studio between shoots or fashion shows to get dresses completely redone or fitted for themselves as well as their shoots. He is a secret weapon. *www.larsnord.com; (212) 727-3832; 203 W. 23rd St., 4th Floor, New York, New York 10011*

TRANSPORTATION

CHAUFFER

Don't drive or don't have a car? If you need to do last-minute market appointments or personal shopping in Los Angeles call the Private Chauffer. The company will take care of your every need. *www.yourdriver.com; (818) 348-3115*

LUGGAGE DELIVERY

Need luggage delivered safe and sound? Don't want to check it on a flight? First Luggage delivers your suitcases to your destination on the date that you request—so you can have it there before or on the day of your arrival! *www.firstluggage.com; (800) 224-5781*

WEB SITES

Altamira

Altamiranyc.blogspot.com

Celebrities have essentially trained themselves to be models. Models still, and always will, have the best personal style no matter what anyone says. If you look carefully, you can see there are similarities between how models dress off-duty and how celebrities dress for lunch at the Ivy on Robertson Boulevard in Los Angeles or while walking the Grove.

Bag Craze

Bagcraze.blogspot.com

This site is amazing because it has every possible "it" bag and every hot line described in no-frills, clean detail.

Bag Snob

Bagsnob.com

Smart and outspoken Tina Craig and Kelly Cook live and die for handbags—and the celebrities who carry them. Here's a typical quote from Tina: "I have always spewed out random thoughts of what I love and hate. I am passionate about calling out hideous five-figure bags because it is an outrage that people are told to buy a piece of crap that has no creativity, style, or any sense! The lesson is to buy what you think is truly beautiful and not what Beyoncé is carrying."

Couture Carrie

Couturecarrie.blogspot.com

I love this site because it's a mix of fashion worldwide, fashion editorial, and trends in one location. It's as if the site took amazing tear sheets and neatly cataloged and presented them in a way that shows what's going on in fashion and accessories, and mixes up all the ideas to make a story.

Daily Front Row

Dailyfrontrow.com

This site keeps you informed about celebrity attendance at shows and includes interviews; business news relating to celebrities, designers, and models signing contracts; party beats; and chic reports. It's a fun place to get all your fashion week updates.

FabSugar

Fabsugar.com

There are many different areas to go into on this site. I love the celebrity coverage as well as beauty, looks, entertainment reports, home, baby, health, money, tech, and pet topics all under one roof.

Fashion Copious

Fashioncopious.typepad.com

This site has all the news you need to know about models: what they're up to, whose covers they're on, what they're wearing in editorials, and, my favorite, a section of quotes available to use and reprint, from William Shakespeare to Miuccia Prada. My favorite is from Imran Ahmed declaring Lady Gaga "the single most powerful editorial machine for fashion designers looking for mass exposure." Pretty great!

Fashion Toast

Fashiontoast.com

Rumi Neely is the owner and operator and has a huge online following. She basically has someone monitor her every move; she posts shots of herself everywhere she goes. At first I thought it was highly self-serving, but I love the way she dresses and the way she looks. She's half Japanese and half Dutch/Scottish and favors OPI's Black Onyx nail polish.

Fashionista

Fashionista.com

This site updates constantly with fashion news as well as job postings for designers, model agents, and the like who need interns.

Fashionologie

Fashionologie.com

I love this site purely because of what founder Tommye Fitzpatrick says in her introduction: "Fashionologie is the musings of a twenty-something American girl who wishes she could have a *Freaky Friday* incident and switch bodies with Phoebe Philo." The site has a great look plus terrific information.

Gaga Daily

Gagadaily.com

I feel confident enough to post this as a great site, which chronicles and details every look and move of Lady Gaga. I feel that she will be around for a long time, as will her style, which will inspire for years to come. Madonna had that power. This one has even more.

Garance Doré

Garancedore.fr/en

Here is a wonderfully intelligent French site that's now available in English. It focuses on beautiful illustrations, fashion, beauty, color, and photography overseas in little snapshots of the founder's life. She grew up reading her mother's glossy magazines and trying on '80s fashion from Thierry Mugler and Azzedine Alaïa, whom everyone from Lady Gaga to Beyoncé to Sandra Bullock to Victoria Beckham seems to love and gravitate toward.

I Lvoe LV

Ilvoelv.com

This is an insanely fabulous love-letter blog to everything Louis Vuitton. The amount of stuff posted on this site astounds me. I've never seen anything like it before. It's so much fun and gets you to the man—Marc Jacobs—who created the "it" bag frenzy when he made the Louis Vuitton Stephen Sprouse graffiti collection of bags and put the idea of waiting lists on the map.

Jak and Jil
Jakandjil.com

This is a wonderful site with photographs of fashionable people and their glorious street styles. I love the writer's point of view and the fact that it works like a chic streetwear blog.

Just Jared
Justjared.buzznet.com

Jared is a great editor. The photos on his site are very informative, and the various angles help show every detail of the celebrities featured. I remember being at an *Us Weekly* event in New York, and Jared was on the side of the red carpet waiting for the celebrities to arrive. When actress Ashley Tisdale saw Jared, she was so happy to see him she screamed out his name. How many times have you heard of that?

My Style
Mystyle.com

For a terrific compilation of the best and worst looks, trends that bark, and rock-and-roll and year-end roundups of great fashion moments, look here. I like the edit and seeing everything at the same time. You get shout-outs, highlights for the week, and all celebrity all the time!

Passion Louboutin
Passionlouboutin.blogspot.com

Updated constantly, this French site tracks celebrities who waltz down the carpet in the most current Christian Louboutin stilettos. It identifies the celebrity and the shoe in picture and in profile so that you can study the heel and the current event.

Red Carpet Fashion Awards
Redcarpet-fashionawards.com

My good friend Catherine Kallon is the creator of this amazing Web site. She is a talented photo editor as well as a brilliant fashion director. She knows her stuff when it comes to the best and worst dressed, celebrities who wear the same outfits, and most-wanted accessories. She is responsible for a vast amount of red carpet coverage in the United States, the United Kingdom, Spain, India, and Asia. She has an amazing eye for detail and a vast knowledge of fashion and designers beyond the obvious players. She knows all about up-and-coming designers such as Prabal Gurung, Altuzarra, and Peter Pilotto. She can identify a look, whether it's on an A-lister or a D-lister. She told me what she does on the site is "focus on what celebrities wear on the red carpet and help my readers find inspiration." I love her humor and how she has no fear of criticizing a look. "Celebrities have such huge support behind them, specifically around these huge events, that they never look anything less than perfect. I think it's great that despite all the resources in the world, sometimes it doesn't work out, for whatever reason. It gives us all hope," Kallon says. Of course, what I especially love is that she's got this amazing British lingo, so even when she's going after someone, it's posh as hell. "As a London girl, I have quite a sarcastic tone, which my readers seem to appreciate!" Hear, hear!

The Sartorialist
Thesartorialist.blogspot.com

Stylist J. Logan Horne tells me that he loves this site because "it's so inspiring from a stylist perspective! Why don't I run into those people on the street? Everyone [else] I see looks like they just rolled out of the dump."

Shoebunny
Shoebunny.com

Want to know who made Charlize Theron's flats? Or want to know when was the last time Jennifer Connelly wore Alessandro Dell'Acqua shoes? Everything is here under one roof: designers, celebrities, a link to shop shoes—around 54,695 to view!—and more. Heaven!

Vogue U.K.
Vogue.co.uk

You'll get excellent fashion news and updates, with a beautiful presentation. The clutter is minimal and you get what you need in nice visuals and scant text. It displays fashion shows, trends, A-list parties, and beauty. I prefer this British edition.

Celebrity Style Guide
Celebritystyleguide.com

This site not only breaks down clothing that celebrities wear on the street but also has detailed descriptions of what characters are wearing on television shows. The site even lists what stores carry these pieces. It has an easy sign-in process, and you can study the designers that young Hollywood gravitates toward, as well as view updates on red carpet looks.

Who What Wear
Whowhatwear.com

Stop here for an amazing, comprehensive, fun, and informative shopping experience. Get highlights about trends on celebrities, designer IDs, and referrals to sites where you can shop the look. I love the tip section, where you're taken into their fashion closet and shown how-tos, which is great for anyone who doesn't know how to pull off a look or style it. If you need to brush up, touch up, and learn a few things, it's all there in living color with references.

INDEX

PHOTO CREDITS